The Time of Your Life

A COMEDY IN THREE ACTS

By William Saroyan

SAMUEL FRENCH, INC.

45 WEST 25TH STREET   NEW YORK 10010

7623 SUNSET BOULEVARD   HOLLYWOOD 90046

LONDON   *TORONTO*

To George Jean Nathan

AN INTRODUCTION TO HIS PLAYS

In the sequence of plays written by me "Love's Old Sweet Song" is the fourth. The first and second are "My Heart's in the Highlands" and "The Time of Your Life." These three plays have been produced in New York and are published in this book. The third and fifth plays, as yet unproduced or unpublished, are "The Hero of the World" and "Something About a Soldier." All of these plays, excepting "My Heart's in the Highlands," were written sometime after March, 1939. A sixth play, "Sweeney in the Trees," was completed on the last day of 1939.

My work has always been the product of my time. Although the world was at peace when I wrote "My Heart's in the Highlands," there was every indication that it would be at war again before long. The poet of this play, Ben Alexander, speaks to the world on the subject of war as follows: "Go ahead. Fire your feeble guns. You won't kill anything. There will always be poets in the world."

The shadow of impending war is over the whole of my second play "The Time of Your Life," and its central character, Joe, spends most of his time examining maps, guns, and the effect of contemporary reality (which includes the constant likelihood of war) on the little and unknown human beings of the world, and on their natural instinct to live gracefully and decently. The Arab of this play says over and over again: "No foundation. All the way down the line."

The theme of my third play, "The Hero of the World," is the effect of this world-disorderliness on both ordinary and superior human beings, canceling the integrity and dignity of the first, and destroying the faith and personal force of the second, leaving man in art speechless, unwilling to act, incapable of accepting responsibility to himself and to society.

"Love's Old Sweet Song" is my fourth play.

I began to write my fifth play, "Something About a Soldier," on September 3, 1939, when it was evident that the war which the world for twenty years had been making inevitable was now to come about. Art and religion would not be able to stop the war any more than they would be able to stop tomorrow. In this play a man of seventy who has lived a truly civilized life, along with his adopted son of eleven, who has not so much as begun to live *consciously* at all, declare war against the political leaders of the world. These two, the old and the young, build a trench in their front yard, put on military uniforms, and *appear* to be making fools of themselves, but only because their foolishness is on a much smaller scale than the historical foolishness of the world. At first the man is regarded as crazy. We, too, at first regard large-scale trouble-makers as crazy. Crazy or sane, however, their persistence, their energy, and the support of millions of simple human beings reduces any aberration in them to something that is irrelevant. And soon after my soldier's declaration of war, his seeming craziness also becomes irrelevant. Since World War II had unquestionably arrived and would unquestionably do its damage, and there was nothing I or you could do about it, I found it necessary to foresee its end and to return to the essential labor of art.

As far as it is possible to do so, in writing my sixth play, "Sweeney in the Trees," I dismissed the war. It had started; consequently it would end. All of us were disgraced once more, and the most (as well as the least) we could do was seek to bring the spirit of man together again.

Wars, for us, are either inevitable, or created. Whatever they are, they should not wholly vitiate art. What art needs is greater men, and what politics needs is better men. If the creation and execution of vast active human projects are necessary for the health of the people, and or the security of the state, they must be the work of men more imaginative than militarists and politicians, and men less fond of their own privacy than artists. Art and politics must move closer together. Reflection and action must be equally valid in good men if history is not to take one course and art another. The weakness of art is that great poems do not ennoble politics, as they certainly should, and the trouble with politics is that they inspire poets only to mockery and scorn.

Art can no longer afford to be contemptuous of politics, and it appears to be time politics took a little instruction from art. Not only is the individual an inhabitant of the world, so also is the nation, and as the world goes, so goes the individual and the nation. What is necessary is greater art in the determining of *how* the world shall go. During this war we have come to accept all manner of artless and base behavior simply because of the tremendous quantity of it in operation. This is historically inevitable. Whatever beauty there may be in a vast military success, it is no beauty that can delight anything in us excepting that which is most uncultivated or inhuman. There is no longer occasion, however, for us to grieve foolishly over the destruction of half a million lives in so short a space of time as twenty days.

We have always believed that art should be one thing, religion one thing, politics one thing, morality one thing, and so on. This kind of isolation of entities, while convenient, is, I believe, foolish. All things must come together as one, which is man. The functioning of all things should be to the glory of living. Art is answerable to politics, and politics is answerable to religion, and all are answerable to man, so that when there is disgrace in life, as there is now, we are *all* guilty, the poet with the statesman, the general with the Pope, and so on. If we can pretend that evil is unnatural or that it is undesirable, all men who are conscious, all functioning men, all men with superior natural endowment, all men of thought, all men of action, all men of faith, must be responsible for the occurrence of evil. Force is the simplest and easiest method in the world by which to settle any kind of dispute. Intelligence and grace, however, are the means of canceling disputes, which are unimaginative *creations*, not realities. Political systems, however deeply and emotionally integrated in the legend and behavior of a people, are worthless when they can survive only at the cost of the actual lives of the people whom they claim to protect. And yet we know one political system or another is still necessary for the management of the world. For this reason, art must enter the arena. It must be *part* of one large thing: the world and its management, life and its instruction. Art must not be a separate and special thing. The intention of art has always been to deepen, extend, elevate, ennoble, strengthen, and refresh the experience of living. It cannot begin to do these things until it accepts part of the management of the *physical* life of man, which is now in the hands of inferior men.

There are many sound arguments in favor of *all* of the things of life and the world, seemingly good or seemingly bad. There is no argument against grace, however, and the way of art, and the companion of art, is grace. This is a word, I think, which must now begin to take the place in our vocabulary of a word long since outworn and for the time being dangerous, if not useless: *truth*. Truth, in our time, has so many variations it has become an actual nonentity. Except statistically, we know no truth, because we have little grace and less honor. There are arguments in favor of war, and I am sure there could be arguments in favor of disease and death. There are times, even in the healthiest of lives, when destruction appears to be more compelling than construction, when death seems more in order than life. Part of the infinite wonder of man is the simultaneous reality of varying and contradictory states. In the flux of inner reality, however, the good and positive appear to be much more abundant and natural than the evil and negative. To have been born is surely our end. To die is beside the point. And to live is our pleasure and law. There may be exhilaration in death, but most of us prefer to survive exhilaration. Most of us cannot help enduring our emotions.

As the conscious individual has intelligence and conscience, in addition to instinct, so also has the *mass*. What it lacks in quality, it makes up in quantity. Simple and relatively uncultivated men of energy who find themselves in the leadership of great masses very often contain within themselves both the intelligence and instinct of the whole mass, plus a compulsion to be somehow superior and immortal. These men are seldom actually evil, although they may seem to be. They are *naïve*. They are not to be scorned or dismissed by men individually superior. While no member of the mass is deprived of his *special* individuality until he dies or is killed, that individuality is so nearly the same as the individuality of millions of others, he and the millions are essentially one, and this one, numbering hundreds of millions, has its model in the *uncultivated* man who is their leader. This man knows which way the mass wishes to go, or can be led, and therein is his superiority — and his essential inferiority. If he leads, he *cannot* lead to anything like a worthy destination, and if he fulfills the wish of the mass, that fulfillment will carry him and the mass to death or disgrace. The instinct of the mass in our time is toward regimentation. Toward the security of narrower limits. The mass appears to be either fearful or unappreciative of the kind of individual freedom the poet, for instance, must insist upon. For the mass this instinct may or may not be proper. Improper or proper, the mass appears to be fearful of exposure to leisure and individual choice. It appears to want the time of its life carefully mapped out and organized, and it appears to want its behavior dictated. (There are good arguments in favor of all this. There are better arguments in favor of truly superior men exerting a truly superior influence.) Without completely abandoning old techniques (which would swiftly bring about even greater chaos), the imperative requirement of our time is to restore faith to the mass and integrity to the individual. The integration of man is still far from realized. In a single age this integration can be immeasurably improved, but it is impossible and useless to seek to imagine its full achievement. Integration will begin to occur when the individual is uninhibited, impersonal, simultaneously natural and cultured, without hate, without fear, and rich in spiritual grace. Strong men of poor, coarse, or undeveloped sensibilities usually find themselves in control of the mass. Strong men of rich sensibilities usually find themselves in control of themselves. This situation would be equitable and satisfactory only if we found it possible to accept as perfectly natural all the kinds of mass behavior which now shock and disgust us. If it were possible or desirable for a man to inhabit only his own personal world, without regard for the lesser (and greater) world of the mass, the present distribution of balance would offend no one. It becomes increasingly true, however, that the most superior man in the world finds a valid variation of himself in the most inferior man in the world, and is hurt by that which hurts this man.

We may feel grateful that the war is on, since we know its beginning is its end, and once again our chance has come to *attempt* the establishment of a not *too* ambitious style of human order, and yet one at least a little finer than the one which created the war. Man wages his wars against himself. It is the same war each of us must wage within himself: good in conflict with evil. In the world the strong are better than the weak only if the strong have love for the weak, and in ourselves virtue is true only if we recognize vice and know it to be an inseparable part of virtue. We cannot begin to be truly good until we know we cannot be *constantly* good. It is hard to imagine anything more likely to be offensive to nature than permanent goodness. What we need is a better proportion of grace and a more generous distribution of understanding.

The majesty of art lies in its simultaneous aloofness and democracy, its *aloneness* and fraternity, and its quietude and tumult. Art begins by being a personal exercise in grace for its creator. Before all others, it refines its maker. The inner calisthenics of art tempers and gives form first to the spirit of the artist. It is the similar affection for and need of form in the many which has carried art into the world, and it is according to the needs of the living that art is given its texture and shape. The first creator of art is one's world and time. The material of art is provided by the world abundantly but chaotically. The labor of art is to take this material and instruct it in grace and form. In ratio to the *rawness* of the material, art exercises its discipline, its precision, and its faith.

Insofar as the world lacks these things, art must provide them. And it must do so blandly, with delight, with ease, and with casualness. It must entertain as it instructs. Its instruction cannot be direct. Since its boundaries are form, and since its cargo is pleasure, in order to accomplish more than the trivial and tentative, art must know deeply and intimately the grief, the despair, and the frustration of its time. It must know the sources of these things and the destinations of them. The source of the grief of man is the monotony of peaceful living. The source of his despair is his lack of resourcefulness and imagination. The source of his frustration is the pain he suffers in the attempt and failure to escape boredom. True escape for man can be provided only by art. To taste life in its full flavor he has not the experience or equipment or style. To accept only as much as he has the equipment to enjoy he has not the discipline or courage. And therefore to evade his defeat, he is eager to enter into any project which provides a substitute somehow or *any*-how for the fullness his dream needed. Such a substitute is participation in war, directly or indirectly, as soldier, instructed, in order, and close to ultimates, murder or death, obvious and immediate triumph or failure; or as bystander, excited by war, pleased, frightened, or fretted. Naturally, when there is war in the world the artist's material in addition to being raw is complex, and very hard to work with. The ecstatic pitch, which art itself seeks to reach, now exists in the world, but is such a base ecstasy that it cannot be given back to the world as great art. What usually happens, therefore, is that artists, at such times, either give up and join the others in bluffing or fretting, or sink deeper and deeper into remoteness and inutility, doing work which is repetitious and beside the point. It is a mistake to imagine that we are *forced* into unpleasant activities, such as war. Our absence of vigilance and industry when there was time to instruct ourselves and the world in alternatives to war is at least partly responsible for the repetition of war. Behavior repeats itself, and great behavior cannot begin to repeat itself until it has *once* occurred, and it cannot begin to occur until art has made it as natural, as easy, and as inevitable as war has been for a long time. *During* a war there is absolutely no chance for correction, just as *after* a gun has been fired there is no chance to deprive its shell of its destination. After the explosion of a gun the most any of us can do is protect our eardrums. We are not forced into unpleasant activities. We either allow them to come about or we encourage them to come about.

There are many who believe art cannot do anything about history. I am not one of these. I believe art can do a good deal about history. Art cannot charge with the infantry or roll along with the armored car units of an army, but there has always been less charging and rolling in history than quietude and conversation; fewer parachute jumps and power dives, less strafing and bombing than poems and the reading of them.

In a time of war if art abandons its labor, war wins its victory, and cheap history tells the fable of the world. If it is impossible for art to reach the soldier who is on the verge of killing or being killed, it can get ready for the soldier's son. If art cannot improve the tone and meaning of the statesman's radio speech, it can anticipate his burial and be ready for his successor. If the world is amuck and there is no one for art to talk to, it can prepare itself for the next generation. War is tentative. Aberration is tentative. Art is not tentative.

It is *true* that as long as there are poets in the world war can kill nothing.

The world now provides art new and more difficult

material. Art has no alternative but to accept this material and to remove from it all foolishness, all feebleness, and all foolish and feeble fantasy.

WILLIAM SAROYAN

San Francisco
June 1, 1940.

NOTE

"The Time of Your Life" was produced by Eddie Dowling in conjunction with The Theatre Guild, and directed by Mr. Dowling and myself. It was first performed in New Haven at the Shubert Theatre, Saturday evening, October 7, 1939. From New Haven it moved to the Plymouth Theatre in Boston for a run of two weeks. It opened in New York at the Booth Theatre on Wednesday, October 25.

This is the cast which opened the play:

THE NEWSBOY	Ross Bagdasarian
THE DRUNKARD	John Farrell
WILLIE	Will Lee
JOE	Eddie Dowling
NICK	Charles De Sheim
TOM	Edward Andrews
KITTY DUVAL	Julie Haydon
DUDLEY	Curt Conway
HARRY	Gene Kelly
WESLEY	Reginald Beane
LORENE	Nene Vibber
BLICK	Grover Burgess
ARAB	Houseley Stevens, Sr.
MARY L.	Celeste Holm
KRUPP	William Bendix
McCARTHY	Tom Tully
KIT CARSON	Len Doyle
NICK'S MA	Michelette Burani
SAILOR	Randolph Wade
ELSIE	Cathie Bailey
A STREET WALKER	Evelyn Geller
HER SIDE KICK	Mary Cheffey

A SOCIETY LADY . . . . Eva Leonard Boyne
A SOCIETY GENTLEMAN . . . . Ainsworth Arnold
FIRST COP . . . . Randolph Wade
SECOND COP . . . . John Farrell

I wish to express my sincere gratitude to each member of the cast.

William Bendix, who plays Krupp, contributed an excellent line to his part, as well as a delightful piece of business, for which I thank him.

The play would not be what it is without the piano-playing, and presence, of Reginald Beane, who plays Wesley; Gene Kelly's hoofing and monologue-reciting as Harry; Manuel Tolegian's off-stage harmonica-playing, for the Arab. My sincere thanks to each of these fine artists.

Charles de Sheim, as Nick, and Edward Andrews, as Tom, improved some of my lines, and Len Doyle, as Kit Carson, introduced pleasant business into his part. My sincere thanks.

My greatest debt of gratitude is to Mr. Dowling, whose great experience in the theater improved the playing of the play throughout.

I must thank Miss Julie Haydon for her splendid portrayal of Kitty Duval. I feel that no other actress in America could give this part the quality Miss Haydon gives it, and the quality which I feel the part should have.

John Farrell, as The Drunkard, made a small role into something, which to me at least, shall always be unforgettable, and Ross Bagdasarian, as The Newsboy, brought youth and foreign-American vigor to another small, but important, part. These two parts were written into the play in Boston, and were expertly performed by these two players almost immediately after the parts were written. My sincere thanks.

The character of Anna, Nick's daughter, although in the play long before the New York opening, was omitted from the cast when the play opened, owing to the fact that in Boston children are not allowed to act on the stage, and there wasn't time enough in New York before the opening to rehearse someone. The part will undoubtedly be in the play by the time this book is published.

There was a good deal of hard work for me to do in getting this play ready for its opening. Even so, because the players were all so capable and enthusiastic, the work was pleasant. I am grateful to everybody.

W. S.

New York
November 1, 1939

PREFACE

Statistics

The first draft was written in six days, in New York, beginning Monday, May 8, 1939, and ending Saturday, May 13. The first title was "The Light Fantastic." There were to have been six acts, one for each day of work. It turned out that the number of acts was five instead of six. Five or six, however, the idea was to write the play in six days. In the number of days of any worker's week. Writers are workers.

George Jean Nathan read the play, liked it and wrote about it in *Newsweek*. Eddie Dowling bought the play.

The writing of the play was, in great part, the consequence of the encouragement of George Jean Nathan and John Mason Brown who voted for "My Heart's in the Highlands," my first play, as the best play of the 1938–1939 season; which, in turn, landed me as a guest at the Drama Critics' Circle Dinner at The Algonquin; which, in another turn, enabled me to meet all the critics who are members of the Circle, as well as Mr. Dowling, who sat across the table from me, and along about ten o'clock at night said, "Any play you write, I'll buy sight unseen." This is the kind of American talk I respect. I asked Mr. Dowling if he was on the level and he assured me that he was. I asked him why, and he told me he believed in my future as a playwright. I felt fine and pretty sure I would have a good play for him very soon, so I began to brag about myself to John Anderson and Tallulah Bankhead and any other critic or actress or playwright who happened to be near by and unable to get away swiftly.

I didn't begin to write the play the next morning because at the time I was living a social life, I began not living a social life the next day, and by Monday, May 8th, I was ready to be a writer again. I began to write.

The idea was also to find out why a writer can't write in New York. What's to stop him? The answer is, of course, nothing. A writer can write anywhere, under any circumstance or complication of circumstances, and nothing's to stop him. He can write well, and he can do it as swiftly as the work involved needs to be done swiftly. In the case of this play it needed to be done very swiftly. The weather was muggy. My room at The Great Northern Hotel had no view, little ventilation, and as soon as possible I wanted to go to Ireland for a long-delayed visit. I also needed money urgently and knew I couldn't earn any unless I had a play to offer Mr. Dowling.

The play was written on a rented Royal Portable Typewriter, which I later bought for $30 from Miss Sophe Rabson, manager of Rabson's, which was across the street from The Great Northern on 56th Street, but is now in a new building, on 52nd Street, and where Miss Rabson graciously allowed me to listen to any phonograph record I cared to listen to, without any obligation; and where a young clerk named Bill was always ready to listen to me on the theme of human nature and so on; and where Miss Rabson's brothers, numbering, I believe, seven, were always pleased to let me watch their television sets and inquire two or three times a day about the cost of new and used Capeharts.

The cigarettes smoked were Chesterfields. The cigars were panatelas. I have forgotten the name of the brand, but they were ten cents straight. The food was Automat food, mainly chicken pie, and occasionally a late supper at the Golden Horn, after which I would sleep an hour or so. The liquor was Scotch.

The play was written night and day. The work did me

good. The social life makes me feel ridiculous after a while. Six days of hard work is all I need to restore me to the pride and dignity of the worker, however.

This work was the first substantial work I had ever done in New York. It was also the longest work I had ever done, anywhere. I felt very good about it. Even if it was a bad play (and I had no reason to believe that it was not a good play), there was nothing lost, nothing to lose, and if the worst came to the worst I was simply broke and would have to borrow money somewhere and go back to San Francisco, instead of visiting Dublin.

Nathan, as I've said, liked the play and Dowling drew up a contract with me and advanced me an enormous sum of money. The title by that time was "The Time of Your Life." I studied the play every now and then and made certain changes in it. I considered other titles, inasmuch as I wasn't sure people wouldn't imagine the play wasn't some fluffy drawing-room comedy. Mr. Nathan's "Sunset Sonata" didn't seem quite right. Certain things were lifted out of the play. New things were put into it. I went to Dublin.

As I write these notes, the play has been revised four or five times, and is still likely to be revised. Even now, there are certain changes I would like to make in my first play, "My Heart's in the Highlands." Everything is there of course, as everything is in a child of three, or a man of thirty, or a man of sixty, but there is always room for refinement.

The World of a Play

Like "My Heart's in the Highlands," "The Time of Your Life" will very likely take an important place in the development of the new American theater. I know why, but I am going to leave the full details to the critics, as I believe in the right of every profession to function. In one dimension I shall probably always understand the play better than anybody else, but in another I shall certainly never understand it as fully as critics, professional or amateur. Every performance of a play varies, if ever so little. Every audience beholding a play varies, if ever so little. Every individual in every audience varies, if ever so little. A play is a world, with its own inhabitants and its own laws and its own values. Although the real world is always essentially the same, it is actually never the same from one hour to another, never exactly the same, so that the same thing today as yesterday, is a different thing, nevertheless. One world furnishes itself to us every morning, and we furnish ourselves to a new world every morning. The world never changes and is always changing, and we in turn never change and are always changing. The world of a play is slightly more secure because considerably less complex, since a play consists of isolation, whereas the world has nothing to be isolated from. The writer of a play himself varies, if ever so little. The parts in a play vary, greatly or less greatly. The people taken from the world and placed in a play vary, greatly superficially, only very little deeply. The players in a play, as themselves, vary considerably.

Unlike the poem, essay, story, or novel, a play is not fully created in itself, as a play. It is not an affair, finally, between one man and one man: the writer and the reader. It becomes fully created only through the deliberate and cultivated functioning of a considerable number of people rehearsed to behave harmoniously and on schedule, so that a desired meaning and message will be conveyed to each individual beholding the play, a meaning which more or less should be the same to all the individuals in the audience.

"The Time of Your Life" is a play of our time. The people in the play are people you are likely to see any day in almost any part of America, certainly at least in certain kinds of American places. Most of the critics said they didn't understand my first play. After a while a few of them turned around and said they did, but on the whole the critics appeared not to like the play because they didn't know why they liked it. I predict that fewer critics this time will need to imagine that they cannot understand this play. I know a few critics won't like it at all, and that many critics will not like all of it.

I don't want this state of affairs to change.

WILLIAM SAROYAN

San Francisco

In the time of your life, live — so that in that good time there shall be no ugliness or death for yourself or for any life your life touches. Seek goodness everywhere, and when it is found, bring it out of its hiding-place and let it be free and unashamed. Place in matter and in flesh the least of the values, for these are the things that hold death and must pass away. Discover in all things that which shines and is beyond corruption. Encourage virtue in whatever heart it may have been driven into secrecy and sorrow by the shame and terror of the world. Ignore the obvious, for it is unworthy of the clear eye and the kindly heart. Be the inferior of no man, nor of any man be the superior. Remember that every man is a variation of yourself. No man's guilt is not yours, nor is any man's innocence a thing apart. Despise evil and ungodliness, but not men of ungodliness or evil. These, understand. Have no shame in being kindly and gentle, but if the time comes in the time of your life to kill, kill and have no regret. In the time of your life, live — so that in that wondrous time you shall not add to the misery and sorrow of the world, but shall smile to the infinite delight and mystery of it.

THE PEOPLE

JOE, a young loafer with money and a good heart
TOM, his admirer, disciple, errand boy, stooge and friend
KITTY DUVAL, a young woman with memories
NICK, owner of Nick's Pacific Street Saloon, Restaurant,
    and Entertainment Palace
ARAB, an Eastern philosopher and harmonica-player
KIT CARSON, an old Indian-fighter
MCCARTHY, an intelligent and well-read longshoreman
KRUPP, his boyhood friend, a waterfront cop who hates
    his job but doesn't know what else to do instead
HARRY, a natural-born hoofer who wants to make peo-
    ple laugh but can't
WESLEY, a colored boy who plays a mean and melan-
    choly boogie-woogie piano
DUDLEY, a young man in love
ELSIE, a nurse, the girl he loves
LORENE, an unattractive woman
MARY L., an unhappy woman of quality and great
    beauty
WILLIE, a marble-game maniac
BLICK, a heel
MA, Nick's mother
A STREET WALKER
HER SIDE KICK
A COP
ANOTHER COP
A SAILOR
A SOCIETY GENTLEMAN
A SOCIETY LADY
THE DRUNKARD
THE NEWSBOY
ANNA, Nick's daughter

THE PLACE

Nick's Pacific Street Saloon, Restaurant, and Entertainment Palace at the foot of Embarcadero, in San Francisco.

A suggestion of room 21 at The New York Hotel, upstairs, around the corner.

THE TIME

Afternoon and night of a day in October, 1939.

The Time of Your Life

ACT ONE

SCENE: *There are swing double doors to the street down*
R. *with steps leading down to barroom; a bar at* R.; *a*
door C. *leading to kitchen; a piano on platform up*
L.C.; *a stage with steps leading up, diagonally in*
upper L., *corner.*

A marble game down R.; *tables and chairs* R., C. *and* L.C.;
a wall telephone up L.C.; *a phonograph down* L.; *a*
chair R. *of door* C.; *table and chairs in back room*
above L. *end of bar.*

At a table L.C., *JOE; always calm, always quiet, always*
thinking, always eager, always bored, always supe-
rior. His expensive clothes are casually and youth-
fully worn and give him an almost boyish appear-
ance. At the moment he is in a sort of Debussy
reverie.

Behind the bar, NICK; a big redheaded Italian with an
enormous naked woman tattooed in red on the inside
of his right arm. He is studying "The Racing Form."

The ARAB, in his place sitting on chair at the end of the
bar. He is a lean old man with a rather ferocious
old-country black moustache, with the ends twisted
up. Between the thumb and forefinger of his left hand
is the Mohammedan tattoo indicating that he has
been to Mecca. He is sipping a glass of beer.

WILLIE, the marble-game maniac, explodes through
the swinging doors R., *and lifts the forefinger of his*
right hand comically, indicating one beer. He is a
very young man, scarcely more than twenty. He is
wearing heavy shoes, a pair of old and dirty cordu-

25

*roys, a light green turtle-neck jersey with a large let-
ter "F" on the chest, an oversize two-button tweed
coat, and a green hat, with the brim up. NICK sets
out a glass of beer for him, he drinks it, straightens up
vigorously, saying, Aaah, makes a solemn face, gives
NICK a one-finger salute of adieu, and begins to
leave, refreshed and restored in spirit. He walks by
the marble game, halts suddenly, turns, studies the
contraption, gestures as if to say, Oh no. Turns to go,
stops, returns to the machine, studies it, takes a
handful of small coins out of his pants pocket, lifts a
nickel, indicates with a gesture, One game, no more.
Puts the nickel in the slot, pushes in the slide, making
an interesting noise.*
The marbles fall, roll, and take their places. He pushes
down the lever, placing one marble in position. Takes
a very deep breath, walks in a small circle, excited at
the beginning of great drama. Stands straight and
pious before the contest. Himself vs. the machine.
Willie vs. Destiny. His skill and daring vs. the cunning and trickery of the novelty industry of America,
and the whole challenging world. He is the last of the
American pioneers, with nothing more to fight but
the machine, with no other reward than lights going
on and off, and six nickels for one. Before him is the
last champion, the machine. He is the last chal-
lenger, the young man with nothing to do in the
world. WILLIE grips the knob delicately, studies the
situation carefully, draws the knob back, holds it a
moment, and then releases it. The first marble rolls
out among the hazards, and the contest is on. At the
very beginning of the play "The Missouri Waltz"*

---

*NOTE: Permission to use this music in production must be obtained
by individual producers from the copyright owner. Contact A.S.C.A.P.
in NYC for details.

is coming from the phonograph. The music ends here. This is the signal for the beginning of the play.

The NEWSBOY comes in.

NEWSBOY. (*cheerfully*) Good-morning, everybody. (*No answer. To NICK:*) Paper, Mister? (*NICK shakes his head, no. The NEWSBOY goes to JOE.*) Paper, Mister? (*JOE shakes his head, no. The NEWSBOY walks away, counting papers.*)

JOE. (*noticing him*) How many you got?

NEWSBOY. Five. (*JOE gives him a bill, takes all the papers, throws them over his head. The NEWSBOY takes money, exits.*)

ARAB. (*picks up papers*) No foundation. All the way down the line.

(*The DRUNK enters R., crosses to the telephone. NICK takes the DRUNK out. The DRUNK returns R.*)

DRUNK. (*champion of the Bill of Rights*) This is a free country, ain't it? (*WILLIE starts upstairs, looks at marble game. Returns.*)

NICK. You can't beat that machine.

WILLIE. Oh, yeah?

JOE. (*calling*)

TOM. (*to himself*) Where the hell is he, every time I need him? (*He looks around calmly: the nickel-in-the-slot phonograph in the corner; the open public telephone; the stage; the marble game; the bar; and so on. He whistles again, this time a little louder.*) Hey, Tom. (*He waits a moment, then whistles again, very loudly.*)

NICK. (*with irritation*) What do you want?

JOE. I want the boy to get me a watermelon, that's what *I* want. What do *you* want? Money, or love, or fame or what? You won't get them studying The Racing Form.

NICK. I like to keep abreast of the times.

(*TOM comes hurrying in* R. *He is a great big man of about thirty or so who appears to be much younger because of the childlike expression of his face: handsome, dumb, innocent, troubled and a little bewildered by everything. He is obviously adult in years, but it seems as if by all rights he should still be a boy. He is defensive as clumsy, self-conscious, overgrown boys are. He is wearing a flashy cheap suit, a Woolworth watch-chain across his vest, and on the little finger of his right hand, a dice-ring: number six. On the middle finger of his left hand a large skull-and-crossbones ring. JOE leans back and studies him with casual disapproval. TOM slackens his pace and becomes clumsy and embarrassed, waiting for the bawling-out he's afraid he's going to get. He crosses to below* L. *of* C. *table.*)

JOE. (*objectively, severely, but warmly*) Who saved your life?

TOM. (*sincerely*) You did, Joe. Thanks.

JOE. How'd I do it?

TOM. (*confused*) What?

JOE. How'd I do it?

TOM. Joe, you know how you did it.

JOE. (softly) I want you to answer me. How'd I save your life? I've forgotten.

TOM. (*remembering, with a big goofy smile*) You made me eat all that chicken soup three years ago when I was sick and hungry.

JOE. (*fascinated*) *Chicken* soup?

TOM. (*eagerly*) Yeah.

JOE. Three years? Is it that long?

TOM. Yeah, sure. 1937. 1938. 1939. This is 1939, Joe.

JOE. Never mind what year it is. Tell me the whole story.

TOM. You took me to the doctor. You gave me money for food and clothes, and paid my room rent. Aw, Joe, you know all the different things you did.

JOE. (*nods, turning away from TOM after each question*) You in good health now?

TOM. Yeah, Joe.

JOE. You got clothes?

TOM. Yeah, Joe.

JOE. (*nods*) You eat three times a day. Sometimes four?

TOM. Yeah, Joe. Sometimes five.

JOE. You got a place to sleep?

TOM. Yeah, Joe.

JOE. (*He nods, pauses, and studies TOM carefully. With terrible irritation:*) Then, where the hell have you been?

TOM. (*humbly*) Joe, I was out in the street listening to the boys. They're talking about the trouble down here on the waterfront.

JOE. (*very sharply*) I want you to be around when I need you.

TOM. (*pleased that the bawling-out is over*) I won't do it again. Joe, one guy out there says there's got to be a revolution before anything will ever be all right.

JOE. (*impatient*) I know all about it. Now, here. Take this money. Go up to the Emporium. You know where the Emporium is?

TOM. Yeah, sure, Joe.

JOE. All right. Take the elevator and go up to the fourth floor. Walk around to the back, to the toy department. Buy me a couple of dollars' worth of toys and bring them here.

TOM. (*amazed*) Toys? What *kind* of toys, Joe?

JOE. Any kind of toys. Little ones that I can put on this table.

TOM. What do you want toys for, Joe?

JOE. (*mildly angry*) *What*?

TOM. All right, all right. You don't have to get sore at *everything*. What'll people think, a big guy like me buying toys?

JOE. *What people*?

TOM. Aw, Joe, you're always making me do crazy things for you, and *I'm* the guy that gets embarrassed. You just sit in this place and make me do all the dirty work.

JOE. (*looking away*) Do what I tell you.

TOM. O.K., but I wish I knew *why*. (*He makes to go, crosses to* R. *below bar.*)

JOE. Wait a minute. Here's a nickel. (*TOM crosses to* R. *of JOE.*) Put it in the phonograph. Number seven. I want to hear that waltz again.

TOM. (*crossing below to phonograph*) Boy, I'm glad *I* don't have to stay and listen to it. Joe, what do you hear in that song anyway? We listen to that song ten times a day. Why can't we hear number six, or two, or nine? There are a lot of other numbers.

JOE. (*emphatically*) Put the nickel in the phonograph. (*pause*) Sit down and wait till the music's over. Then go get me some toys.

TOM. O.K. O.K.

JOE. (*loudly*) Never mind being a martyr about it either. The cause isn't worth it.

(*TOM puts the nickel into the machine, with a ritual of impatient and efficient movement which plainly shows his lack of sympathy or enthusiasm. His manner also reveals, however, that his lack of sympathy is*

*spurious and exaggerated. Actually, he is fascinated
by the music, but is so confused by it that he tries to
pretend he dislikes it. The MUSIC begins. TOM
turns chair* L. *of* L.C. *table and sits up stage. It is
another variation of the "Missouri Waltz," played
dreamily and softly, with perfect orchestral form, and
with a theme of weeping in the horns repeated a
number of times. At first TOM listens with something close to irritation, since he cannot understand
what is so attractive in the music to JOE, and so
painful and confusing to himself. Very soon, however, he is carried away helplessly by the melancholy
story of grief and nostalgia in the stubborn, flowing
rhythm. He stands quarreling with the grief and confusion in himself. JOE, on the other hand, listens as if
he were not listening, indifferent and unmoved. What
he's interested in is TOM. He turns and glances at
TOM. KITTY DUVAL, who lives in a room in The
New York Hotel, around the corner, comes beyond
the swinging doors* R. *quietly, and walks slowly to the
bar, her reality and rhythm a perfect accompaniment
to the sorrowful American music, which is* her *music,
as it is TOM's, which the world drove out of her,
putting in its place brokenness and all manner of
spiritually crippled forms. She seems to understand
this, and is angry; angry with herself, full of hate for
the poor world, and full of pity and contempt for its
tragic, unbelievable, confounded people. She is a
small powerful girl, with that kind of delicate and
rugged beauty which no circumstance of evil or ugly
reality can destroy. This beauty is that element of the
immortal which is in the seed of good and common
people, and which is kept alive in some of the female
of our kind, no matter how accidentally or pointlessly
they may have entered the world. KITTY DUVAL is*

somebody. There is an angry purity, and a fierce
pride, in her. In her stance, and way of walking, there
is grace and arrogance.)

KITTY. (*goes to bar*) Beer. (*NICK places a glass of beer*
before her mechanically. She swallows half the drink, and
listens to the music again. TOM turns and sees her. He
becomes dead to everything in the world but her. He
stands like a lump, fascinated and undone by his almost
religious adoration for her. JOE notices him.)

JOE. (*gently*) Tom. (*TOM begins to move toward the*
bar, where KITTY is standing. Loudly.) Tom. (*TOM*
halts, then turns, and JOE motions to him to come over to
the table. TOM goes over. Quietly.) Have you got everything straight?

TOM. (*out of the world, crossing down L. of JOE*)
What?

JOE. What do you mean, what? I just gave you some
instructions.

TOM. (*pathetically*) What do you want, Joe?

JOE. I want you to come to your senses. (*He stands up*
quietly and knocks TOM's hat off.)

TOM. (*picks up his hat quickly*) I got it, Joe. I got it.
The Emporium. Fourth floor. In the back. The toy department. Two dollars' worth of toys. That you can put
on a table.

KITTY. (*to herself*) Who the hell is he to push a big
man like that around?

JOE. I'll expect you back in a half hour. Don't get
side-tracked anywhere. Just do what I tell you.

TOM. (*pleading*) Joe? Can't I bet four bits on a horse
race? There's a long shot—Precious Time—that's
going to win by ten lengths. I got to have money. (*JOE*
points to the street. TOM crosses below and goes out R.
NICK is combing his hair, looking in the mirror.)

NICK. I thought you wanted him to get you a watermelon.

JOE. I forgot. (*to KITTY, clearly, slowly, with great compassion*) What's the dream?

KITTY. (*moving to JOE, coming to*) What?

JOE. (*holding the dream for her*) What's the dream, now?

KITTY. (*coming still closer*) What dream?

JOE. What dream! The dream you're dreaming.

NICK. Suppose he did bring you a watermelon? What the hell would you do with it?

JOE. (*irritated*) I'd put it on this table. I'd look at it. Then I'd eat it. What do you *think* I'd do with it, sell it for a profit?

NICK. How should I know what *you'd* do with *anything*? What I'd like to know is, where do you get your money from? What work do you do?

JOE. (*looking at KITTY*) Bring us a bottle of champagne.

KITTY. (*at R. of JOE's table*) Champagne?

JOE. (*simply*) Would you rather have something else?

KITTY. What's the big idea?

JOE. I thought you might like some champagne. I myself am very fond of it.

KITTY. Yeah, but what's the big idea? You can't push me around.

JOE. (*gently but severely*) It's not in my nature to be unkind to another human being. I have only contempt for wit. Otherwise I might say something obvious, therefore cruel, and perhaps untrue.

KITTY. You be careful what you think about me.

JOE. (*slowly, not looking at her*) I have only the noblest thoughts for both your person, and your spirit.

NICK. (*having listened carefully and not being able to make it out*) What are you talking about?

KITTY. You shut up. You—

JOE. He owns this place. He's an important man. All kinds of people come to him looking for work. Comedians. Singers. Dancers.

KITTY. I don't care. He can't call me names.

NICK. All right, sister. I know how it is with a two-dollar whore in the morning.

KITTY. Don't you dare call me names. I used to be in burlesque.

NICK. (*profoundly, as it were*) If you were ever in burlesque, I used to be Charlie Chaplin.

KITTY. (*swallowing beer*) I *was* in burlesque. I played the burlesque circuit from coast to coast. I've had flowers sent to me by European royalty. I've had dinner with young men of wealth and social position.

NICK. You're dreaming.

KITTY. (*to JOE*) *I was in burlesque.* Kitty Duval. That was my name. Lifesize photographs of me in costume in front of burlesque theaters all over the country.

JOE. (*gently, coaxingly*) I believe you. Have some champagne.

NICK. (*going above her to* L. *of JOE's table, with champagne*) There he goes again.

JOE. Miss Duval?

KITTY. (*sincerely; going over to chair* L. *of JOE's table, sits*) That's not my *real* name. That's my *stage* name.

JOE. I'll call you by your stage name.

NICK. (*pouring*) All right, sister, make up your mind. Are you going to have champagne with him, or not?

JOE. Pour the lady some wine.

NICK. O.K., Professor. Why you come to this joint instead of one of the high-class dumps uptown is more than I can understand. Why don't you have champagne at the St. Francis? Why don't you drink with a lady?

KITTY. (*furiously*) Don't you call me names—you dentist.

JOE. Dentist?

NICK. (*amazed, loudly*) What kind of cussing is that? (*pause; looking at KITTY, then at JOE, bewildered*) This guy doesn't belong here. The only reason I've got champagne is because *he* keeps ordering it all the time. (*to KITTY*) Don't think you're the only one he drinks champagne with. He drinks with *all* of them. (*pause*) He's crazy. Or something.

JOE. (*confidentially*) Nick, I think you're going to be all right in a couple of centuries.

NICK. I'm sorry, I don't understand your English. (*He takes JOE's hat and hangs it on hook up L. JOE lifts his glass. KITTY slowly lifts hers.*)

JOE. (*putting everything he's got into it*) To the spirit, Kitty Duval.

KITTY. (*beginning to understand, and very grateful, looking at him*) Thank you. (*They drink.*)

JOE. (*calling*) Nick.

NICK. Yeah?

JOE. Would you mind putting a nickel in the machine again? Number—

NICK. Seven. I know. I know. I don't mind at all, Your Highness, although, personally, I'm not a lover of music. (*going above table to the phonograph*) As a matter of fact I think Tchaikowsky was a dope.

JOE. Tchaikowsky? Where'd you ever hear of Tchaikowsky?

NICK. He was a dope.

JOE. Yeah. Why?

NICK. They talked about him on the radio one Sunday morning. He was a sucker. He let a woman drive him crazy.

JOE. I see.

NICK. I stood behind that bar listening to the God damn stuff and cried like a baby. *None but the lonely heart!* He was a dope.

JOE. What made you cry?

NICK. What?

JOE. (*sternly*) What made you cry, Nick?

NICK. (*angry with himself*) I don't know.

JOE. I've been underestimating you, Nick. Play number seven.

NICK. They get everybody worked up. They give everybody stuff they shouldn't have. (*NICK puts the nickel into the machine and the Waltz begins again. He listens to the music, then studies The Racing Form.*)

KITTY. (*to herself, dreaming*) I like champagne, and everything that goes with it. Big houses with big porches, and big rooms with big windows, and big lawns, and big trees, and flowers growing everywhere, and big shepherd dogs sleeping in the shade.

NICK. (*crossing below toward stairs* R.) I'm going next door to Frankie's to make a bet. I'll be right back.

JOE. Make one for me.

NICK. (*stopping* R. *of JOE*) Who do you like?

JOE. (*giving him money*) Precious Time.

NICK. *Ten dollars?* Across the board?

JOE. No. On the nose.

NICK. O.K. (*He goes out* R.)

(*DUDLEY R. BOSTWICK, as he calls himself, breaks through the swinging doors* R., *and pratically flings himself upon the open telephone. DUDLEY is a young man of about twenty-four or twenty-five, ordinary and yet extraordinary. He is smallish, as the saying is, neatly dressed in bargain clothes, over-*

worked and irritated by the routine and dullness and monotony of his life, apparently nobody and nothing, but in reality a great personality. The swindled young man. Educated, but without the least real understanding. A brave, dumb, salmon-spirit struggling for life in weary, stupefied flesh, dueling ferociously with a banal mind which has been only irritated by what it has been taught. He is a great personality because, against all these handicaps, what he wants is simple and basic: a woman. This urgent and violent need, common yet miraculous enough in itself, considering the unhappy environment of the animal, is the force which evaluates him from nothingness to greatness. A ridiculous greatness, but in the nature of things beautiful to behold. All that he has been taught, and everything he believes, is phony, and yet he himself is real, almost super-real, because of this indestructible force in himself. His face is ridiculous. His personal rhythm is tense and jittery. His speech is shrill and violent. His gestures are wild. His ego is disjointed and epileptic. And yet deeply he possesses the same wholeness of spirit, and directness of energy, that is in all species of animals. There is little innate or cultivated spirit in him, but there is no absence of innocent animal force. He is a young man who has been taught that he has a chance, as a person, and believes it. As a matter of fact, he hasn't a chance in the world, and should have been told by somebody, or should not have had his natural and valuable ignorance spoiled by education, ruining an otherwise perfectly good and charming member of the human race. At the telephone he immediately begins to dial furiously, hangs up furiously, and furiously begins to

turn the pages of the telephone book, looking for the right number. Not more than half a minute after the firecracker arrival of DUDLEY R. BOSTWICK, occurs the polka-and-waltz arrival of HARRY, R.
HARRY is another story. He comes in timidly, turning about uncertainly, awkward, out of place everywhere, embarrassed and encumbered by the contemporary costume, sick at heart, but determined to fit in somewhere. His arrival constitutes a dance. His clothes don't fit. The pants are a little too large. The coat, which doesn't match, is also·a little too large, and loose. He is a dumb young fellow, but he has ideas. A philosophy, in fact. His philosophy is simple and beautiful. The world is sorrowful. The world needs laughter. HARRY is funny. The world needs HARRY. HARRY will make the world laugh. He has probably had a year or two of high school. He has also listened to the boys at the pool room. He's looking for NICK. He goes to the ARAB, and says, "Are you Nick?" The ARAB shakes his head. He stands at the bar, waiting. He waits very busily.)

HARRY. (*as NICK returns*) You Nick?

NICK. (*very loudly*) I am *Nick.*

HARRY. (*acting*) Can you use a great comedian?

NICK. (*behind the bar*) Who, for instance?

HARRY. (*almost angry*) Me.

NICK. You? What's funny about you? (*DUDLEY at the telephone, is dialing. Because of some defect in the apparatus the dialing is very loud.*)

DUDLEY. Hello. Sunset 7349? May I speak to Miss Elsie Mandelspiegel? (*pause*)

HARRY. (*with spirit and noise, dancing*) I dance and do gags and stuff.

NICK. In costume? Or are you wearing your costume?

DUDLEY. All I need is a cigar.

KITTY. I'd walk out of the house, and stand on the porch, and look at the trees, and smell the flowers, and run across the lawn, and lie down under a tree, and read a book. A book of poems, maybe.

DUDLEY. (*very, very clearly*) Elsie Mandelspiegel. (*impatiently*) She has a room on the fourth floor. She's a nurse at the Southern Pacific Hospital. Elsie Mandelspiegel. She works at night. Elsie. Yes. (*He begins waiting again.*)

(*WESLEY, a colored boy, comes from* R. *to the bar and stands near HARRY, waiting.*)

NICK. Beer?

WESLEY. No, sir. I'd like to talk to you.

NICK. (*to HARRY*) All right. Get funny.

HARRY. (*getting funny, an altogether different person, an actor with great energy, both in power of voice, and in force and speed of physical gesture*) Now, I'm standing on the corner of Third and Market. I'm looking around. I'm figuring it out. There it is. Right in front of me. The whole city. The whole world. People going by. They're going somewhere. I don't know where, but they're going. I ain't going *anywhere*. Where the hell can you go? I'm figuring it out. All right, I'm a citizen. A fat guy bumps his stomach into the face of an old lady. They were in a *hurry. Fat* and old. *They bumped.* Boom. I don't know. It may mean war. *War.* Germany. England. Russia. I don't know for sure. (*Loudly, dramatically, he salutes, about faces, presents arms, aims, and fires.*) WAAAAAR. (*He blows a call to arms. NICK gets sick of this, indicates with a gesture that HARRY should hold it, and goes to WESLEY.*)

NICK. What's on *your* mind?

WESLEY. (*confused*) Well —

NICK. Come on. Speak up. Are you hungry, or what?

WESLEY. Honest to God, I ain't hungry. All I want is a job. I don't want no charity.

NICK. Well, what can you do, and how good are you?

WESLEY. I can run errands, clean up, wash dishes, anything.

DUDLEY. (*on the telephone, very eagerly*) Elsie? Elsie, this is Dudley. Elsie, I'll jump in the bay if you don't marry me. Life isn't worth living without you. I can't sleep. I can't think of anything but you. All the time. Day and night and night and day. Elsie, I love you. I love you. What? (*burning up*) Is this Sunset 7-3-4-9? *7943*? (*calmly, while WILLIE begins making a small racket*) Well, what's *your* name? *Lorene*? Lorene Smith? I thought you were Elsie Mandelspiegel. What? Dudley. Yeah. Dudley R. Bostwick. Yeah. R. It stands for Raoul, but I never spell it out. I'm pleased to meet *you*, too. What? There's a lot of noise around here. (*WILLIE stops hitting the marble game*) Where am I? At Nick's, on Pacific Street. I work at the S. P. I told them I was sick and they gave me the afternoon off. Wait a minute. I'll ask them. I'd like to meet *you*, too. Sure. I'll ask them. (*turns around to NICKS*) What's this address?

NICK. Number 3 Pacific Street, you cad.

DUDLEY. Cad? You don't know how I've been suffering on account of Elsie. I take things too ceremoniously. I've got to be more lackadaisical. (*into telephone*) Hello, Elenore? I mean, Lorene. It's number 3 Pacific Street. Yeah. Sure. I'll wait for you. How'll you know me? You'll *know* me. I'll recognize *you*. Good-bye, now. (*He hangs up, crosses to table R. and sits.*)

HARRY. (*continuing his monologue, with gestures,*)

movements, and so on) I'm standing there. I didn't do anything to anybody. Why should *I* be a soldier? (*sincerely, insanely*) BOOOOOOOOOM. *WAR!* O.K. War. *I* retreat. *I* hate war. I move to Sacramento.

NICK. (*shouting*) All right, Comedian. Lay off a minute.

HARRY. (*broken-hearted, going to WILLIE*) Nobody's got a sense of humor any more. The world's dying for comedy like never before, but nobody knows how to *laugh*.

NICK. (*to WESLEY*) Do you belong to the union?

WESLEY. What union?

NICK. For the love of Mike, where've you been? Don't you know you can't come into a place and ask for a job and get one and go to work, just like that. You've got to belong to one of the unions.

WESLEY. I didn't know. I got to have a job. Real soon.

NICK. Well, you've got to belong to a union.

WESLEY. I don't want any favors. All I want is a chance to earn a living.

NICK. Go on into the kitchen and tell Sam to give you some lunch.

WESLEY. Honest, I ain't hungry.

DUDLEY. (*shouting*) What I've gone through for Elsie. (*NICK comes from behind bar and gives him a beer.*)

HARRY. I've got all kinds of funny ideas in my head to help make the world happy again. (*WESLEY almost faints from hunger. NICK catches him just in time. The ARAB and NICK go off with WESLEY into the kitchen.*)

NICK. (*holding WESLEY*) No, he isn't hungry.

HARRY. (*to WILLIE*) See if you think this is funny. It's my own idea. I created this dance myself. It comes after the monologue. (*HARRY begins to dance. WILLIE watches a moment, and then goes back to the game.*

It's a goofy dance, which HARRY does with great sorrow, but much energy.)

DUDLEY. Elsie. Aw, gee, Elsie. What the hell do I want to see Lorene Smith for? Some girl I don't know. (*JOE and KITTY have been drinking in silence. There is no sound now except the soft shoe shuffling of HARRY, the Comedian. ARAB re-enters and sits in chair.*)

JOE. What's the dream now, Kitty Duval?

KITTY. (*dreaming the words and pictures*) I dream of home. Christ, I always dream of home. I've no *home.* I've no place. But I always dream of all of us together again. We had a farm in Ohio. There was nothing good about it. It was always sad. There was always trouble. But I always dream about it as if I could go back and Papa would be there and Mamma and Louie and my little brother Stephen and my sister Mary. I'm Polish. Duval! My name isn't Duval, it's Koranovsky. Katerina Koranovsky. We lost everything. The house, the farm, the trees, the horses, the cows, the chickens. Papa died. He was old. He was thirteen years older than Mamma. We moved to Chicago. We tried to work. We tried to stay together. Louie got in trouble. The fellows he was with killed him for something. I don't know what. Stephen ran away from home. Seventeen years old. I don't know where he is. Then Mamma died. (*pause*) What's the dream? I dream of home. (*NICK comes out of the kitchen with WESLEY who sits at the piano.*)

NICK. Here. Sit down here and rest. That'll hold you for a *while.* Why didn't you tell me you were hungry? You all right now?

WESLEY. Yes, I am. Thank you. I didn't know I was *that* hungry.

NICK. (*to L. of piano*) Fine. (*to HARRY who is dancing*) Hey. What the hell do you think you're doing?

HARRY. (*stopping*) That's my own idea. I'm a natural-born dancer and comedian. (*WESLEY begins slowly, one note, one chord at a time, to play the piano.*)

NICK. (*going to back of bar*) You're no good. Why don't you try some other kind of work? Why don't you get a job in a store, selling something? What do you want to be a comedian for?

HARRY. (*to upper end of bar*) I've got something for the world and they haven't got sense enough to let me give it to them. Nobody knows me.

DUDLEY. Elsie. Now I'm waiting for some dame I've never seen before. Lorene Smith. Never saw her in my life. Just happened to get the wrong number. She turns on the personality, and I'm a cooked Indian. Give me a beer, please.

HARRY. Nick, you've got to see my act. It's the greatest thing of its kind in America. (*NICK comes to DUDLEY with beer. HARRY follows him.*) All I want is a chance. No salary to begin. Let me try it out tonight. If I don't wow 'em, O.K., I'll go home. If vaudeville wasn't dead, a guy like me would have a chance.

NICK. (*He crosses up behind bar. HARRY follows him.*) You're not funny. You're a sad young punk. What the hell do you want to try to be funny for? You'll break everybody's heart. What's there for you to be funny about? You've been poor all your life, haven't you?

HARRY. I've been poor all right, but don't forget that some things count more than some other things.

NICK. What counts more, for instance, than what else, for instance?

HARRY. Talent, for instance, counts more than money, for instance, that's what, and I've got talent. I get new ideas night and day. Everything comes natural to me. I've got style, but it'll take me a little time to round it out. That's all. (*By now WESLEY is playing something of his own which is very good and out of the world. He plays about half a minute, after which HARRY begins to dance.*)

NICK. (*watching*) I run the lousiest dive in Frisco, and a guy arrives and makes me stock up with champagne. The whores come in and holler at me that they're ladies. Talent comes in and begs me for a chance to show itself. Even society people come here once in a while. I don't know what for. Maybe it's liquor. Maybe it's the location. Maybe it's my personality. Maybe it's the crazy personality of the joint. The old honky-tonk. (*pause*) Maybe they can't feel at home anywhere else. (*By now WESLEY is really playing, and HARRY is going through a new routine. DUDLEY grows sadder and sadder.*)

KITTY. Please dance with me.

JOE. (*loudly*) I never learned to dance.

KITTY. Anybody can dance. Just hold me in your arms.

JOE. I'm very fond of you. I'm *sorry*. I *can't* dance. I wish to God I could.

KITTY. Oh, please.

JOE. Forgive me. I'd like to very much. (*KITTY dances alone. TOM comes in R. with a package. He sees KITTY and goes ga-ga again. He comes out of the trance and puts the bundle on the L.C. table in front of JOE. NICK comes to above JOE's table, gets bottle and glasses and returns to back of bar.*)

JOE. (*taking the package*) What'd you get?

TOM. Two dollars' worth of toys. That's what you sent me for. The girl asked me what I wanted with toys. I didn't know what to tell her. (*He turns and looks at KITTY.*) Joe? I've got to have some money. After all you've done for me, I'll do anything in the world for you, but, Joe, you got to give me some money once in a while.

JOE. What do you want it for? (*TOM turns and stares at KITTY dancing.*)

JOE. (*noticing*) Sure. Here. Here's five. (*shouting*) Can you dance?

TOM. (*proudly*) I got second prize at the Palomar in Sacramento five years ago.

JOE. (*loudly, opening package*) O.K., dance with her.

TOM. You mean *her*?

JOE. (*loudly*) I mean Kitty Duval, the burlesque queen. I mean the queen of the world burlesque. Dance with her. She wants to dance.

TOM. (*helpless*) Joe, can I tell you something?

JOE. (*He brings out a toy and winds it.*) You don't have to. I know. You love her. You *really* love her. I'm not blind. I know. But take care of yourself. Don't get sick that way again.

NICK. (*looking at and listening to WESLEY with amazement*) Comes in here and wants to be a dishwasher. Faints from hunger. And then sits down and plays better than Heifetz.

JOE. Heifetz plays the violin.

NICK. All right, don't get careful. He's good, ain't he?

TOM. (*to KITTY*) Kitty.

JOE. (*He lets the toy go, loudly.*) Don't *talk.* Just *dance.*

(*TOM and KITTY dance. NICK is at the bar, watching everything. HARRY is dancing. DUDLEY is grieving into his beer. LORENE SMITH, about thirty-seven, very overbearing and funny-looking, comes to the bar from R.*)

NICK. What'll it be, lady?

LORENE. (*looking about and scaring all the young men*) I'm looking for the young man I talked to on the telephone. Dudley R. Bostwick.

DUDLEY. (*jumping, running to her, stopping, shocked*) Dudley R. (*slowly*) Bostwick? Oh, yeah. He left here ten minutes ago. You mean Dudley Bostwick, that poor man on crutches?

LORENE. Crutches?

DUDLEY. Yeah. Dudley Bostwick. That's what he *said* his name was. He said to tell you not to wait.

LORENE. Well. (*She begins to go, turns around.*) Are you sure *you're* not Dudley Bostwick?

DUDLEY. Who — me? (*grandly*) My name is Roger Tenefrancia. I'm a French-Canadian. I never saw the poor fellow before.

LORENE. It seems to me your voice is like the voice I heard over the telephone.

DUDLEY. A coincidence. An accident. A quirk of fate. One of those things. Dismiss the thought. That poor cripple hobbled out of here ten minutes ago.

LORENE. (*crossing to door* R.) He said he was going to commit suicide. I only wanted to be of help. (*She goes out* R.)

DUDLEY. Be of help? What kind of help could she be, of? (*DUDLEY runs to the telephone in the corner.*) Gee whiz, Elsie. Gee whiz. I'll never leave you again. (*He turns the pages of a little address book.*) Why do I always forget the number? I've tried to get her on the phone a hundred times this week and I still forget the number. She won't come to the phone, but I keep trying anyway. She's out. She's not in. She's working. I get the wrong number. Everything goes haywire. I can't sleep. (*defiantly*) She'll come to the phone one of these days. If there's anything to true love at all, she'll come to the phone. Sunset 7349. (*He dials the number, as JOE goes on studying the toys. They are one big mechanical toy, whistles, and a music box. JOE blows into the whistles, quickly, by way of getting casually acquainted with them. TOM and KITTY stop dancing. TOM stares at her.*)

DUDLEY. Hello. Is this Sunset 7349? May I speak to Elsie? Yes. (*emphatically, and bitterly*) No, this is *not* Dudley Bostwick. This is Roger Tenefrancia of Montreal, Canada. I'm a childhood friend of Miss Mandelspiegel. We went to kindergarten together. (*hand over phone*) God damn it. (*into phone*) Yes. I'll wait, thank you.

TOM. I love you. (*leading KITTY to below door* R.)

KITTY. You want to go to my room? (*TOM can't answer.*) Have you got two dollars?

TOM. (*shaking his head with confusion*) I've got *five* dollars, but I *love* you.

KITTY. (*looking at him*) You want to spend *all* that money? (*TOM embraces her. They go out* R. *JOE watches, goes back to the toy.*)

JOE. Where's that longshoreman, McCarthy?

NICK. He'll be around.

JOE. What do you think he'll have to say today?

NICK. (*coming around bar*) Plenty, as usual. I'm going next door to see who won that third race at Laurel.

JOE. Precious Time won it.

NICK. That's what you think. (*He goes out* R.)

JOE. (*to himself*) A horse named McCarthy is running in the sixth race today.

DUDLEY. (*on the phone*) Hello. Hello, Elsie? Elsie? (*His voice weakens; also his limbs.*) My God. She's come to the phone. Elsie, I'm at Nick's on Pacific Street. You've got to come here and talk to me. Hello. Hello, Elsie? (*amazed*) Did she hang up? Or was I disconnected? (*He hangs up and goes to bar. WESLEY is still playing the piano. HARRY is still dancing. JOE has wound up the big mechanical toy and is watching it work.*)

NICK. (*returns from* R.; *goes to* R. *of JOE, watching the toy*) Say. That's some gadget.

JOE. How much did I win?

NICK. How do you know you *won*?

JOE. Don't be silly. He said Precious Time was going to win by ten lengths, didn't he? He's in love, isn't he?

NICK. (*handing JOE money*) O.K. I don't know why, but Precious Time won. You got eighty for ten. How do you do it?

JOE. (*roaring*) Faith. Faith. How'd he win?

NICK. By a nose. Look him up in The Racing Form. The slowest, the cheapest, the worst horse in the race, and the worse jockey. What's the matter with my luck?

JOE. How much did you lose?

NICK. Fifty cents.

JOE. You should never gamble.

NICK. Why not?

JOE. You always bet fifty cents. You've got no more faith than a flea, that's why.

HARRY. (*shouting*) How do you like this, Nick? (*He is really busy now, all legs and arms.*)

NICK. (*turning and watching, crossing above to piano*) Not bad. Hang around. You can wait table. (*to WESLEY*) Hey. Wesley. Can you play that again tonight?

WESLEY. (*turning, but still playing the piano*) I don't know for sure, Mr. Nick. I can play *something*.)

NICK. Good. *You* hang around, too. (*He goes behind the bar.*)

(*The atmosphere is now one of warm, natural, American*

ease; every man innocent and good; each doing what he believes he should do, or what he must do. There is deep American naïveté and faith in the behavior of each person. No one is competing with anyone else. No one hates anyone else. Every man is living, and letting live. Each man is following his destiny as he feels it should be followed; or is abandoning it as he feels it must, by now, be abandoned; or is forgetting it for the moment as he feels he should forget it. Although everyone is dead serious, there is unmistakable smiling and humor in the scene; a sense of the human body and spirit emerging from the world-imposed state of stress and fretfulness, fear and awkwardness, to the more natural state of casualness and grace. Each person belongs to the environment, in his own person, as himself: WESLEY is playing better than ever. HARRY is hoofing better than ever. NICK is behind the bar shining glasses. JOE is smiling at the toy and studying it. DUDLEY, although still troubled, is at least calm now and full of melancholy poise. WILLIE, at the marble-game, is happy. The ARAB is deep in his memories, where he wants to be. Into this scene and atmosphere comes BLICK from R. BLICK is the sort of human being you dislike at sight. He is no different from anybody else physically. His face is an ordinary face. There is nothing obviously wrong with him, and yet you know that it is impossible, even by the most generous expansion of understanding, to accept him as a human being. He is the strong man without strength—strong only among the weak—the weakling who uses force on the weaker. BLICK enters casually, as if he were a customer, and immediately HARRY begins slowing down.)

BLICK. (*oily, and with mock-friendliness*) Hello, Nick.

NICK. (*stopping his work and leaning across the bar*) What do you want to come here for? You're too big a man for a little honky-tonk.

BLICK. (*flattered*) Now, Nick.

NICK. Important people never come here. *Here.* Have a drink. (*puts out whiskey bottle and glass*)

BLICK. Thanks, I don't drink.

NICK. (*drinking the whiskey himself*) Well, why don't you?

BLICK. I have responsibilities.

NICK. You're head of the lousy Vice Squad. There's no vice here.

BLICK. (*sharply*) Street-walkers are working out of this place.

NICK. (*angry*) What do you want?

BLICK. (*loudly*) I just want you to know that it's got to stop. (*The music stops. The mechanical toy runs down. There is absolute silence, and a strange fearfulness and disharmony in the atmosphere now. HARRY doesn't know what to do with his hands or feet. WESLEY's arms hang at his sides. JOE quietly pushes the toy to one side of the table eager to study what is happening. WILLIE stops playing the marble-game, turns around and begins to wait. DUDLEY straightens up very, very vigorously, as if to say: "Nothing can scare me. I know love is the only thing." The ARAB is the same as ever, but watchful. NICK is arrogantly aloof. There is a moment of this silence and tension, as though BLICK were waiting for everybody to acknowledge his presence. He is obviously flattered by the acknowledgement of HARRY, DUDLEY, WESLEY, and WILLIE, but a little irritated by NICK's aloofness and unfriendliness.*)

NICK. Don't look at me. I can't tell a street-walker from a lady. You married?

BLICK. You're not asking *me* questions. *I'm* telling *you*.

NICK. (*interrupting*) You're a man of about forty-five or so. You *ought* to know better.

BLICK. (*angry*) Street-walkers are working out of this place.

NICK. (*beginning to shout*) Now, don't start any trouble with me. People come here to drink and loaf around. I don't care who they are.

BLICK. Well, I do.

NICK. The only way to find out if a lady is a street-walker is to walk the streets with her, go to bed, and make sure. You wouldn't want to do that. You'd *like* to, of course.

BLICK. Any more of it, and I'll have your joint closed.

NICK. (*very casually, without ill-will*) Listen. I've got no use for you, or anybody like you. You're out to change the world from something bad to something worse. Something like yourself.

BLICK. (*furious pause, and contempt*) I'll be back to-night. (*He begins to go* R.)

NICK. (*very angry but very calm*) Do yourself a big favor and don't come back tonight. Send somebody else. I don't like your personality.

BLICK. Don't break any laws. I don't like yours, either. (*He looks the place over, and goes out* R. *There is a moment of silence. Then WILLIE turns and puts a new nickel in the slot and starts a new game. WESLIE turns to the piano and rather falteringly begins to play. His heart really isn't in it. HARRY walks about, unable to dance. DUDLEY lapses into his customary melancholy, at a table. NICK whistles a little: suddenly stops. JOE winds the toy)*

JOE. (*comically*) Nick. You going to kill that man?

NICK. I'm disgusted.

JOE. Yeah? Why?

NICK. Why should I get worked up over a guy like that? Why should I hate *him*? He's nothing. He's nobody. He's a mouse. But every time he comes into this place I get burned up. He doesn't want to drink. He doesn't want to sit down. He doesn't want to take things easy. Tell me one thing?

JOE. Do my best.

NICK. What's a punk like *that* want to go out and try to change the world for?

JOE. (*amazed*) Does *he* want to change the world, too?

NICK. (*irritated*) You know what I mean. What's he want to bother people for? He's *sick.*

JOE. (*almost to himself, reflecting on the fact that BLICK too wants to change the world*) I guess he wants to change the world at that.

NICK. So I go to work and hate him.

JOE. It's not him, Nick. It's everything.

NICK. Yeah, *I know.* But I've still got no use for him. He's *no good.* You know what I mean? He hurts little people. (*confused*) One of the girls tried to commit suicide on account of him. (*furiously*) I'll break his head if he hurts anybody around here. This is *my* joint. (*afterthought*) Or anybody's *feelings,* either.

(*WARN curtain*)

JOE. He may not be so bad, deep down underneath.

NICK. I know all about him. He's no good. (*During this talk WESLEY has really begun to play the piano, the*

*toy is rattling again, and little by little HARRY has begun
to dance. NICK has come around the bar, and now, very
much like a child — forgetting all his anger — is watching
the toy work. He begins to smile at everything; turns and
listens to WESLEY; watches HARRY; nods at the
ARAB; shakes his head at DUDLEY and gestures ami-
ably about WILLIE. It's his joint all right. It's a good,
low-down, honky-tonk American place that lets people
alone.*)

NICK. (*crossing to chair L. of C. table*) I've got a good
joint. There's nothing wrong here. Hey. Comedian. Stick
to the dancing tonight. I think you're O.K. (*HARRY
goes to telephone and dials.*) Wesley? Do some more of
that tonight. That's fine!

HARRY. Thanks, Nick. Gosh, I'm on my way at last.
(*on telephone*) Hello, Ma? Is that you, Ma? Harry. I got
the job. (*He hangs up and walks around, smiling.*)

NICK. (*watching the toy all this time*) Say, that really is
something. What is that, anyway?

(*MARY L. comes in R.*)

JOE. (*holding it toward NICK, and MARY L.*) Nick,
this is a toy. A contraption devised by the cunning of
man to drive boredom, or grief, or anger out of children.
A noble gadget. A gadget, I might say, infinitely nobler
than any other I can think of at the moment. (*EVERY-
BODY gathers around JOE's table to look at the toy. The
toy stops working. JOE winds the music box, lifts a whistle; blows it, making a very strange, funny and sorrowful
sound.*) Delightful. Tragic, but delightful. (*WESLEY
plays the music-box theme on the piano. MARY L. takes
a table C.*)

NICK. Joe. That girl, Kitty. What's she mean, calling

me a dentist? I wouldn't hurt anybody, let alone a tooth. (*NICK goes to MARY L.'s table. HARRY imitates the toy, dances. The piano music comes up, and the LIGHT dims slowly, while the piano solo continues.*)

CURTAIN

ACT TWO

*NICK's, an hour later. All the people who were there
when the Curtain came down are still there. DUD-
LEY at table* R., *ARAB seated up* R. *HARRY and
WESLEY at piano. JOE at his table, quietly shuffling and turning a deck of cards, and at the same
time watching the face of the WOMAN, and looking
at the initials on her handbag as though they were the
symbols of the lost glory of the world. At table* C.,
*WOMAN, in turn, very casually regards JOE,
occasionally—or rather senses him; has sensed him
in fact the whole hour. She is mildly tight on beer, and
JOE himself is tight, but as always, completely under
control; simply sharper. The OTHERS are about, at
tables, and so on.*

JOE. Is it Madge—Laubowitz?

MARY. Is what *what*?

JOE. Is the name Mabel Lepescu?

MARY. What name?

JOE. The name the initials M. L. stand for. The initials
on your bag.

MARY. No.

JOE. (*after a long pause, thinking deeply what the
name might be, turning a card, looking into the beautiful
face of the WOMAN*) Margie Longworthy?

MARY. (*All this is very natural and sincere, no comedy
on the part of the people involved, they are both solemn,
being drunk.*) No.

JOE. (*his voice higher-pitched, as though he were growing a little alarmed*) Midge Laurie? (*MARY shakes her
head.*) My initials are J. T.

MARY. (*pause*) John?

55

JOE. No. (*pause*) Martha Lancaster?

MARY. No. (*slight pause*) Joseph?

JOE. Well, not exactly. That's my first name, but everybody calls me Joe. The last name is the tough one. I'll help you a little I'm Irish. Is it just plain Mary?

MARY. Yes, it is. I'm Irish, too. At least on my father's side. English on my mother's side.

JOE. I'm Irish on both sides. Mary's one of my favorite names. I guess that's why I didn't think of it. I met a girl in Mexico City named Mary once. She was an American from Philadelphia. She got married there. In Mexico City, I mean. While I was *there.* We were in love, too. At least *I* was. You never know about anyone else. They were engaged, you see, and her mother was with her, so they went through with it. Must have been six or seven years ago. She's probably got three or four children by this time.

MARY. Are you still in love with her?

JOE. Well—no. To tell you the truth, I'm not sure. I guess I am. I didn't even know she was engaged until a couple of days before they got married. I thought *I* was going to marry her. I kept thinking all the time about the kind of kids we would be likely to have. My favorite was the third one. The first two were fine. Handsome and fine and intelligent, but that third one was different. Dumb and goofy-looking. I liked *him* a lot. When she told me she was going to be married, I didn't feel so bad about the first two, it was that dumb one.

MARY. (*after a pause of some few seconds*) What do you do?

JOE. Do? To tell you the truth, nothing.

MARY. Do you always drink a great deal?

JOE. (*scientifically*) Not *always.* Only when I'm awake. I sleep seven or eight hours every night, you know.

MARY. How nice. I mean to drink when you're awake.

JOE. (*thoughtfully*) It's a privilege.

MARY. Do you really *like* to drink?

JOE. (*positively*) As much as I like to *breathe.*

MARY. (*beautifully*) Why?

JOE. (*dramatically*) Why do I like to drink? Because I don't like to be gypped. Because I don't like to be dead most of the time and just a little alive every once in a long while. (*pause*) If I don't drink, I become fascinated by unimportant things — like everybody else. I get busy. Do things. All kinds of little stupid things, for all kinds of little stupid reasons. Proud, selfish, *ordinary* things. I've done them. Now I don't do anything. *I live all the time.* Then I go to sleep.

MARY. Do you sleep well?

JOE. (*taking it for granted*) Of course.

MARY. (*quietly, almost with tenderness*) What are your plans?

JOE. (*loudly, but also tenderly*) Plans? I haven't *got* any. *I just get up.*

MARY. (*beginning to understand everything*) Oh, yes. Yes, of course. (*DUDLEY puts a nickel in the phonograph.*)

JOE. (*thoughtfully*) Why do I drink? (*Pause, while he thinks about it. The thinking appears to be profound and complex, and has the effect of giving his face a very comical and naïve expression.*) That question calls for a pretty complicated answer. (*He smiles abstractly.*)

MARY. Oh, I didn't mean —

JOE. (*swiftly, gallantly*) No. No. I *insist.* I *know* why. It's just a matter of finding words. Little ones.

MARY. It really doesn't matter.

JOE. (*seriously*) Oh, yes it does. (*clinically*) Now, why do I drink? (*scientifically*) No. Why does *anybody* drink? (*working it out*) Every day has twenty-four hours.

MARY. (*sadly, but brightly*) Yes, that's true.

JOE. Twenty-four hours. Out of the twenty-four hours at *least* twenty-three and a half are — my God, I don't know why — dull, dead, boring, empty, and murderous. Minutes on the clock, *not time of living.* It doesn't make any difference who you are or what you do, twenty-three and a half hours of the twenty-four are spent *waiting.*

MARY. Waiting?

JOE. (*gesturing, loudly*) And the more you wait, the less there is to wait *for.*

MARY. (*attentively, beautifully his student*) Oh?

JOE. (*continuing*) That goes on for days and days, and weeks and months and years, and years, and the first thing you know *all* the years are dead. All the minutes are dead. You yourself are dead. There's nothing to wait for any more. Nothing except *minutes* on the *clock.* No time of life. Nothing but minutes, and idiocy. Beautiful, bright, intelligent idiocy. (*pause*) Does that answer your question?

MARY. (*earnestly*) I'm afraid it does. Thank you. You shouldn't have gone to all the trouble.

JOE. No trouble at all. (*pause*) You have children?

MARY. Yes. Two. A son and a daughter.

JOE. (*delighted*) How swell. Do they look like you?

MARY. Yes.

JOE. Then why are you sad?

MARY. I was always sad. It's just that after I was married I was allowed to drink.

JOE. (*eagerly*) Who are you waiting for?

MARY. No one.

JOE. (*smiling*) I'm not waiting for anybody, either.

MARY. My husband, of course.

JOE. Oh, sure.

MARY. He's a lawyer.

JOE. (*standing, leaning on the table.*) He's a great guy. I like him. I'm very fond of him.

MARY. (*listening*) You have responsibilities?

JOE. (*loudly; rises*) *One*, and *thousands*. As a matter of fact, I feel responsible to everybody. At least to everybody I meet. I've been trying for three years to find out if it's possible to live what I think is a civilized life. I mean a life that can't hurt any other life.

MARY. You're famous?

JOE. Very. Utterly unknown, but very famous. Would you like to dance?

MARY. All right.

JOE. (*loudly*) I'm *sorry*. I don't dance. I didn't think *you'd* like to.

MARY. To tell you the truth, I don't like to dance at all.

JOE. (*proudly; commentator*) I can hardly walk.

MARY. You mean you're tight?

JOE. (*smiling*) No. I mean *all* the time.

MARY. (*sitting forward*) Were you ever in Paris?

JOE. In 1929, and again in 1934.

MARY. What month of 1934?

JOE. Most of April, all of May, and a little of June.

MARY. I was there in November and December that year.

JOE. We were there almost at the same time. You were married?

MARY. Engaged. (*They are silent a moment, looking at one another. Quietly and with great charm:*) Are you *really* in love with me?

JOE. Yes.

MARY. Is it the champagne?

JOE. Yes. Partly, at least. (*He sits down.*)

MARY. If you don't see me again, will you be very unhappy?

JOE. Very.

MARY. (*getting up*) I'm so pleased. (*JOE is deeply grieved that she is going. In fact, he is almost panic-stricken about it, getting up in a way that is full of furious sorrow and regret.*) I must go now. Please don't get up. (*JOE is up, staring at her with amazement.*) Good-by.

JOE. (*simply*) Good-by.

(*Music ends. The WOMAN stands looking at him a moment, then turns and goes slowly out R. JOE stands staring after her for a long time. Just as he is slowly sitting down again, the NEWSBOY enters R., and goes to JOE's table.*)

NEWSBOY. Paper, Mister?

JOE. How many you got this time?

NEWSBOY. Eleven. (*JOE buys them all, looks at all, throws them away. ARAB crosses, picks up one and returns to his seat up R. The NEWSBOY looks at JOE, shakes head, goes to bar. Troubled:*) Hey, Mister, do you own this place?

NICK. I own this place.

NEWSBOY. Can you use a great lyric tenor?

NICK. (*almost to himself*) Great lyric tenor? (*loudly*) Who?

NEWSBOY. Me. I'm getting too big to sell papers. I don't want to holler headlines all the time. I want to *sing*. You can use a great lyric tenor, can't you?

NICK. What's lyric about you?

NEWSBOY. (*voice high-pitched, confused*) My voice.

NICK. Oh. (*slight pause, giving in*) All right, then — sing! (*The NEWSBOY breaks into swift and beautiful song: "When Irish Eyes Are Smiling." NICK and JOE listen carefully: NICK with wonder, JOE with amazement and delight.*)

NEWSBOY. (*singing*)
When Irish eyes are smiling,
Sure 'tis like a morn in Spring.
In the lilt of Irish laughter,
You can hear the angels sing.
When Irish hearts are happy,
All the world seems bright and gay.
But when Irish eyes are smiling—

NICK. (*loudly, swiftly*) Are you Irish?

NEWSBOY. (*speaking swiftly, loudly, a little impatient with the irrelevant question*) No. I'm Greek. (*He finishes the song, singing louder than ever.*) Sure they steal your heart away. (*He turns to NICK dramatically, like a vaudeville singer begging his audience for applause. NICK studies the boy eagerly. JOE gets to his feet and leans toward the BOY and NICK.*)

NICK. Not bad. Let me hear you again about a year from now.

NEWSBOY. (*thrilled*) Honest?

NICK. Yeah. Along about November 7th, 1940.

NEWSBOY. (*happier than ever before in his life, running over to JOE*) Did you hear it too, Mister?

JOE. Yes, and it's great. What part of Greece?

NEWSBOY. Salonica. Gosh, Mister. Thanks.

JOE. Don't wait a year. Come back with some papers a little later. You're a great singer.

NEWSBOY. (*thrilled and excited*) Aw, thanks, Mister. So long. (*running, to NICK*) Thanks, Mister. (*He runs out* R. *JOE and NICK look at the swinging doors. JOE sits down. NICK laughs.*)

NICK. Joe, people are so wonderful. Look at that kid.

JOE. Of course they're wonderful. Every one of them is wonderful.

(*MCCARTHY and KRUPP come in* R., *talking.*)

MCCARTHY is a big man in work clothes, which make him seem very young. He is wearing black jeans, and a blue workman's shirt, no tie, no hat. He has broad shoulders, a lean intelligent face, thick black hair. In his right back pocket is the longshoreman's hook. His arms are long and hairy. His sleeves are rolled up to just below his elbows. He is a casual man, easy-going in movement, sharp in perception, swift in appreciation of charm or innocence or comedy, and gentle in spirit. His speech is clear and full of warmth. His voice is powerful, but modulated. He enjoys the world, in spite of the mess it is, and he is fond of people, in spite of the mess they are.

KRUPP is not quite as tall or broad-shouldered as MCCARTHY. He is physically encumbered by his uniform, club, pistol, belt, and cap and he is plainly not at home in the role of policeman. His movement is stiff and unintentionally pompous. He is a naïve man, essentially good. His understanding is less than MCCARTHY's, but he is honest and he doesn't try to bluff.)

KRUPP. You don't understand what I mean. Hi-ya, Joe. (*crossing up to* C. *of bar*)

JOE. Hello, Krupp.

MCCARTHY. (*crossing to above KRUPP*) Hi-ya, Joe.

JOE. Hello, McCarthy.

KRUPP. Two beers, Nick. (*to MCCARTHY*) All I do is carry out orders, carry out orders. I don't know what the idea is behind the order. Who it's for, or who it's against, or why. All I do is carry it out. (*NICK gives them beer.*)

MCCARTHY. You don't read enough.

KRUPP. I do read. I read *The Examiner* every morning. *The Call-Bulletin* every night.

MCCARTHY. And carry out orders. What are the orders now?

KRUPP. To keep the peace down here on the waterfront.

MCCARTHY. Keep it for who? (*to JOE*) Right?

JOE. (*sorrowfully*) Right.

KRUPP. How do I know for who? The peace. Just keep it.

MCCARTHY. It's got to be kept for somebody. Who would you suspect it's kept for?

KRUPP. (*thinking*) For citizens!

MCCARTHY. I'm a citizen!

KRUPP. All right, I'm keeping it for you.

MCCARTHY. By hitting me over the head with a club? (*to JOE*) Right?

JOE. (*melancholy, with remembrance*) I don't know.

KRUPP. Mac, you know I never hit you over the head with a club.

MCCARTHY. But you will if you're on duty at the time and happen to stand on the opposite side of myself, on duty.

KRUPP. We went to Mission High together. We were always good friends. The only time we ever fought was that time over Alma Haggerty. Did *you* marry Alma Haggerty? Right?

JOE. Everything's right.

MCCARTHY. No. Did you? (*to JOE*) Joe, are you with me or against me?

JOE. I'm with everybody. One at a time.

KRUPP. No. And that's just what I mean.

MCCARTHY. You mean neither one of us is going to marry the thing we're fighting for?

KRUPP. *I don't even know what it is.*

MCCARTHY. You don't read enough, I tell you.

KRUPP. Mac, you don't know what you're fighting for, either.

MCCARTHY. It's so simple, it's fantastic.

KRUPP. All right, what are you fighting for?

MCCARTHY. For the rights of the inferior. Right?

JOE. Something like that.

KRUPP. The who?

MCCARTHY. The inferior. The world full of Mahoneys who haven't got what it takes to make monkeys out of everybody else, near by. The men who were created equal. Remember?

KRUPP. Mac, you're not inferior.

MCCARTHY. I'm a longshoreman. And an idealist. I'm a man with too much brawn to be an intellectual, exclusively. (*crossing to* R. *of JOE*) I married a small, sensitive, cultured woman so that my kids would be sissies instead of suckers. A strong man with any sensibility has no choice in this world but to be a heel, or a *worker*. I haven't the heart to be a heel, so I'm a worker. I've got a son in high school who's already thinking of being a writer.

KRUPP. I wanted to be a writer once.

JOE. Wonderful. (*He puts down the paper, looks at KRUPP and MCCARTHY.*)

MCCARTHY. They *all* wanted to be writers. Every maniac in the world that ever brought about the murder of people through war started out in an attic or a basement writing poetry. It stank. So they got even by becoming important heels. And it's still going on.

KRUPP. Is it really, Joe?

JOE. Look at today's paper.

MCCARTHY. Right now on Telegraph Hill is some punk who is trying to be Shakespeare. Ten years from now he'll be a senator. Or a communist.

KRUPP. Somebody ought to do something about it.

McCARTHY. (*mischievously, with laughter in his voice*) The thing to do is to have more magazines. Hundreds of *them. Thousands.* Print everything they write, so they'll believe they're immortal. That way keep them from going haywire.

KRUPP. Mac, you ought to be a writer yourself.

McCARTHY. I hate the tribe. They're mischief-makers. Right?

JOE. (*swiftly*) Everything's right. Right and wrong.

KRUPP. Then why do you read?

McCARTHY. (*laughing*) It's relaxing. It's soothing. (*pause*) The lousiest people born into the world are writers. Language is all right. It's the people who use language that are lousy. (*The ARAB has moved a little closer, and is listening carefully. To the ARAB:*) What do you think, Brother?

ARAB. (*at first step down* R; *after making many faces, thinking very deeply*) No foundation. All the way down the line. What. What-not. Nothing. I go walk and look at sky. (*He goes out* R.)

KRUPP. (*follows to below bar*) What? What-not? (*to JOE*) What's that mean?

JOE. (*slowly, thinking, remembering*) What? What-not? That means this side, that side. Inhale, exhale. What: birth. What-not: death. The inevitable, the astounding, the magnificent seed of growth and decay in all things. Beginning, and end. That man, in his own way, is a prophet. He is one who, with the help of *beer*, is able to reach that state of deep understanding in which what and what-not, the reasonable and the unreasonable, are *one.*

McCARTHY. Right.

KRUPP. If you can understand that kind of talk, how can you be a longshoreman?

McCARTHY. I come from a long line of McCarthys

who never married or slept with anything but the most powerful and quarrelsome flesh. (*He drinks beer.*)

KRUPP. I could listen to you two guys for hours, but I'll be damned if I know what the hell you're talking about.

MCCARTHY. The consequence is that all the McCarthys are too great and too strong to be heroes. Only the weak and unsure perform the heroic. They've *got* to. The more heroes you have, the worse the history of the world becomes. Right?

JOE. Go outside and look at it.

KRUPP. You sure can philos — philosoph — Boy, you can talk.

MCCARTHY. I wouldn't talk this way to anyone but a man in uniform, and a man who couldn't understand a word of what I was saying. The party I'm speaking of, my friend, is *YOU.* (*The phone rings.*) (*HARRY gets up from his table suddenly and begins a new dance.*)

KRUPP. (*noticing him, with great authority*) Here. Here. What do you think you're doing?

HARRY. (*stopping*) I just got an idea for a new dance. I'm trying it out. Nick, Nick, the phone's ringing. (*NICK goes to phone.*)

KRUPP. (*to McCarthy*) Has he got a right to do that?

MCCARTHY. The living have danced from the beginning of time. I might even say, the dance and the life have moved along together, until now we have — (*to HARRY*) Go into your dance, son, and show us what we have.

HARRY. I haven't got it worked out *completely* yet, but it starts out like this. (*He dances.*)

NICK. (*on phone*) Nick's Pacific Street Restaurant, Saloon, and Entertainment Palace. Good afternoon. Nick speaking. (*listens*) Who? (*turns around*) Is there a Dudley Bostwick in the joint? (*DUDLEY jumps to his feet and goes to phone. NICK goes to up of bar.*)

DUDLEY. (*on phone*) Hello. Elsie? (*listens*) You're coming down? (*elated; to the saloon*) She's coming down. (*pause*) No. I won't drink. Aw, gosh, Elsie. (*He hangs up, looks about him strangely, as if he were just born, walks around touching things, putting chairs in place, and so on.*)

McCARTHY. (*to HARRY*) Splendid. Splendid.

HARRY. Then I go into this little routine. (*He demonstrates.*)

KRUPP. Is that good, Mac?

McCARTHY. It's awful, but it's honest and ambitious, like everything else in this great country.

HARRY. Then I work along into this. (*He demonstrates.*) And *this* is where I *really* get going. (*He finishes the dance.*)

McCARTHY. Excellent. A most satisfying demonstration of the present state of the American body and soul. (*crossing to HARRY and shaking his hand*) Son, you're a genius.

HARRY. (*delighted*) I go on in front of an audience for the first time in my life tonight.

McCARTHY. They'll be delighted. Where'd you learn to dance?

HARRY. Never took a lesson in my life. I'm a natural-born dancer. And *comedian*, too.

McCARTHY. (*astounded*) You can make people *laugh*?

HARRY. (*dumbly*) I can be funny, but they won't laugh.

McCARTHY. That's odd. Why not?

HARRY. I don't know. They just won't laugh.

McCarthy. Would you care to be funny now?

Harry. I'd like to try out a new monologue I've been thinking about.

McCarthy. Please do. I promise you if it's funny I shall *roar* with laughter.

Harry. This is it. (*goes into the act, with much energy*) I'm up at Sharkey's on Turk Street. It's a quarter to nine, daylight saving. Wednesday, the eleventh. What I've got is a headache and a 1918 nickel. What I *want* is a cup of coffee. If I buy a cup of coffee with the nickel, I've got to walk home. I've got an eight-ball problem. George the Greek is shooting a game of snooker with Pedro the Filipino. *I'm in rags.* They're wearing thirty-five dollar suits, made to order. I haven't got a cigarette. They're smoking Bobby Burns panatelas. I'm thinking it over, like I always do. George the Greek is in a tough spot. If I buy a cup of coffee, I'll want another cup. What happens? My *ear* aches! My ear. George the Greek takes the cue. Chalks it. Studies the table. Touches the cue-ball delicately. Tick. What happens? He makes the three-ball! What do I do? I get confused. *I go out and buy a morning paper.* What the hell do I want with a morning paper? What I *want* is a cup of coffee, and a good used car. I go out and buy a morning paper. Thursday, the twelfth. Maybe the headline's about *me.* I take a quick look. *No. The headline is not about me.* It's about Hitler. Seven thousand miles away. I'm here. Who the hell is Hitler? Who's behind the eight-ball? I turn around. *Everybody's behind the eight-ball*! (*Pause. KRUPP moves toward HARRY as if to make an important arrest. HARRY moves to the swinging doors. MCCARTHY stops KRUPP.*)

McCarthy. It's the funniest thing I've ever heard. Or *seen*, for that matter.

Harry. Then, why don't you laugh?

McCARTHY. I don't know, *yet.*

HARRY. I'm always getting funny ideas that nobody will laugh at.

McCARTHY. It may be that you've stumbled headlong into a new kind of comedy.

HARRY. Well, what good is it if it doesn't make anybody laugh?

McCARTHY. There are *kinds* of laughter, son. I must say, in all truth, that I *am* laughing, although not *out loud.*

HARRY. I want to *hear* people laugh. *Out loud.* That's why I keep thinking of funny things to say.

McCARTHY. (*crossing below to down* R.) Well. They may catch on in time. Let's go, Krupp. So long, Joe. (*MCCARTHY and KRUPP go out* R.)

JOE. So long. (*after a moment's pause*) Hey, Nick.

NICK. Yeah. (*HARRY exits rear* C. *DUDLEY goes to bar and gets beer.*)

JOE. Bet McCarthy in the last race.

NICK. You're crazy. That horse is a double-crossing, no good —

JOE. Bet everything you've got on McCarthy.

NICK. I'm not betting a nickel on him. *You* bet everything you've got on McCarthy.

JOE. I don't need money.

NICK. What makes you think McCarthy's going to win?

JOE. McCarthy's name's McCarthy, isn't it?

NICK. Yeah, So what?

JOE. The *horse* named McCarthy is going to win, *that's all.* Today.

NICK. Why?

JOE. You do what I tell you, and everything will be all right.

NICK. McCarthy likes to talk, that's all. Where's Tom?

JOE. He'll be around. He'll be miserable, but he'll be around. Five or ten minutes more.

NICK. You don't believe that Kitty, do you? About being in burlesque?

JOE. (*very clearly*) I believe dreams sooner than statistics.

NICK. (*remembering*) She sure is somebody. Called me a dentist. (*TOM, turning about, confused, troubled, comes in, R., and hurries to JOE's table.*)

JOE. What's the matter?

TOM. (*giving JOE money*) Here's your five, Joe. I'm in trouble again.

JOE. If it's not organic, it'll cure itself. If it *is* organic, science will cure it. What is it, organic or non-organic?

TOM. Joe, I don't know — (*He sits at R. of table, buries his head on his arms and seems to be completely broken-down.*)

JOE. What's eating you? I want you to go on an errand for me.

TOM. It's Kitty.

JOE. What about her?

TOM. She's up in her room, crying.

JOE. Crying?

TOM. Yeah, she's been crying for over an hour. I been talking to her all this time, but she won't stop.

JOE. What's she crying about?

TOM. I don't know. I couldn't understand anything. She kept crying and telling me about a big house and collie dogs all around and flowers and one of her brother's dead and the other lost somewhere. Joe, I can't stand Kitty crying.

TOM. You want to marry the girl?

TOM. (*nodding*) Yeah.

JOE. (*curious and sincere*) Why?

TOM. I don't know why, exactly, Joe. (*pause*) Joe, I

don't like to think of Kitty out in the streets. I guess I love her, that's all.

JOE. She's a nice girl.

TOM. She's like an angel. She's not like those other streetwalkers.

JOE. (*swiftly*) Here. Take all this money and run next door to Frankie's and bet it on the nose of McCarthy.

TOM. (*swiftly*) All this money, Joe? McCarthy?

JOE. Yeah, hurry.

TOM. (*going*) Ah, Joe. If McCarthy wins we'll be rich.

JOE. Get going, will you? (*TOM runs out R. and nearly knocks over the ARAB coming back in. NICK fills him a beer without a word.*)

ARAB. No foundation, anywhere. Whole world. No foundation. All the way down the line.

NICK. (*angry*) McCarthy! Just because you got a little lucky this morning, you have to go to work and throw away eighty bucks.

JOE. He wants to marry her.

NICK. Suppose she doesn't want to marry *him*?

JOE. (*amazed*) Oh, yeah. (*thinking*) Now, why wouldn't she want to marry a nice guy like Tom?

NICK. She's been in burlesque. She's had flowers sent to her by European royalty. She's dined with young men of quality and social position. She's above Tom.

TOM. (*comes running in, crossing to JOE, disgusted*) They were running when I got there. Frankie wouldn't take the bet. McCarthy didn't get a call till the stretch. I thought we were going to save all this money. Then McCarthy won by *two* lengths.

JOE. What'd he pay, fifteen to one?

TOM. Better, but Frankie wouldn't take the bet.

NICK. (*throwing a dish towel across the room*) Well, for the love of Mike.

JOE. Give me the money.

Tom. (*giving back the money*) We would have had about a thousand five hundred dollars.

Joe. (*pause; bored, displeased*) Go up to Schwabacher-Frey and get me the biggest Rand-McNally map of the nations of Europe they've got. On your way back stop at one of the pawn shops on Third Street, and buy me a good revolver and some cartridges.

Tom. She's up in her room crying, Joe.

Joe. Go get me those things.

Nick. (*crossing below to c. table, gets glasses*) What are you going to do, study the map, and then go out and shoot somebody?

Joe. I want to read the names of some European towns and rivers and valleys and mountains.

Nick. What do you want with the revolver? (*goes to back of bar, dries glasses*)

Joe. I want to study it. I'm interested in things. Here's twenty dollars, Tom. Now go get them things.

Tom. A big map of Europe. And a revolver.

Joe. Get a good one. Tell the man you don't know anything about firearms and you're trusting him not to fool you. Don't pay more than ten dollars.

Tom. Joe, you got something on your mind. Don't go fool with a revolver.

Joe. Be sure it's a good one.

Tom. Joe.

Joe. What, Tom?

Tom. Joe, what do you send me out for crazy things for all the time?

Joe. They're not crazy, Tom. Now, get going.

Tom. What about Kitty, Joe?

Joe. Let her cry. It'll do her good.

Tom. If she comes in here while I'm gone, talk to her, will you Joe? Tell her about me.

JOE. O.K. Get going. Don't load that gun. Just buy it and bring it here.

TOM. (*going to stair landing,* R.) You won't catch me loading any gun.

JOE. Wait a minute. Take these toys away.

TOM. (*crossing to* R. *of JOE*) Where'll I take them?

JOE. Give them to some kid. No. Take them up to Kitty. Toys stopped me from crying once. That's the reason I had you buy them. I wanted to see if I could find out *why* they stopped me from crying. I remember they seemed awfully stupid at the time.

TOM. Shall I, Joe? Take them up to Kitty? Do you think they'd stop *her* from crying?

JOE. They might. You get curious about the way they work and you forget whatever it is you're remembering that's making you cry. That's what they're for.

TOM. Yeah. Sure. The girl at the store asked me what I wanted with toys. I'll take them up to Kitty. (*tragically*) She's like a little girl. (*He goes out* R.)

WESLEY. Mr. Nick, can I play the piano again?

NICK. Sure. Practice all you like — until I tell you to stop.

WESLEY. You going to pay me for playing the piano?

NICK. Sure. I'll give you enough to get by on.

WESLEY. (*amazed and delighted*) Get money for playing the piano? (*He goes to the piano and begins to play quietly. HARRY goes up on the little stage and listens to the music. After a while he begins a soft shoe dance which is very quiet and relaxing.*)

NICK. What were you crying about?

JOE. My mother.

NICK. What about her?

JOE. She was dead. I stopped crying when they gave me the toys.

(*NICK'S MOTHER, a little old woman of sixty or so,
dressed plainly in black, her face shining, comes in
briskly, chattering loudly in Italian, gesturing. NICK
is delighted to see her.*)

NICK'S MOTHER. (*in Italian*) Everything all right,
Nickie?

NICK. (*in Italian*) Sure, Mamma. (*NICK'S MOTHER
leaves as gaily and as noisily as she came.*)

JOE. Who was that?

NICK. (*to JOE, proudly and a little sadly*) My mother.
(*still looking at the swinging doors*)

JOE. What'd she say?

NICK. Nothing. Just wanted to see me. What do you
want with that gun?

JOE. I study things, Nick.

(*An old man who looks like KIT CARSON staggers in* R.,
*looks around; edges to bar; reaction to NICK; goes
above to* L. *and moves about aimlessly and finally
goes to chair* L. *of* C. *table*)

KIT CARSON. Murphy's the name. Just an old trapper.
Mind if I sit down?

JOE. Be delighted. What'll you drink?

KIT CARSON. (*sitting down*) Beer. Same as I've been
drinking. And thanks.

JOE. (*to NICK*) Glass of beer, Nick. (*NICK brings the
beer to the table, and goes back of bar. KIT CARSON
swallows it in one swig, wipes his big white mustache with
the back of his right hand.*)

KIT CARSON. (*moving in*) I don't suppose you ever fell
in love with a midget weighing thirty-nine pounds?

JOE. Can't say that I have, but have another beer.

KIT CARSON. (*intimately*) Thanks, thanks. Down in Gallup, twenty years ago. Fellow by the name of Rufus Jenkins came to town with six white horses and two black ones. Said he wanted a man to break the horses for him because his left leg was wood and he couldn't do it. Had a meeting at Parker's Mercantile Store and finally came to blows, me and Henry Walpal. Bashed his head with a brass cuspidor and ran away to Mexico, but he didn't die. (*SAILOR enters R. and goes to bar.*) Couldn't speak a word. Took up with a cattle-breeder named Diego, educated in California. Spoke the language better than you and me. Said, Your job, Murph, is to feed them prize bulls. I said, Fine, what'll I feed them? He said, Hay, lettuce, salt, beer, and aspirin. Came to blows two days later over an accordion he claimed I stole. I had *borrowed* it. During the fight I busted it over his head; ruined one of the finest accordions I ever saw. Grabbed a horse and rode back across the border. Texas. Got to talking with a fellow who looked honest. Turned out to be a Ranger who was looking for me. (*KILLER enters R, sits D.S. of bar.*)

JOE. Yeah. You were saying, a thirty-nine pound midget.

KIT CARSON. Will I ever forget that lady? Will I ever get over that amazon of small proportions?

JOE. Will you?

KIT CARSON. If I live to be sixty.

JOE. Sixty? You look more than sixty now.

KIT CARSON. That's trouble showing in my face. Trouble and complications. I was fifty-eight three months ago.

JOE. That accounts for it, then. Go ahead, tell me more.

KIT CARSON. Told the Texas Ranger my name was Rothstein, mining engineer from Pennsylvania, looking for something worth while. Mentioned two places in Houston. Nearly lost an eye early one morning, going down the stairs. (*rises*) Ran into a six-footer with an iron-claw where his right hand was supposed to be. Said, You broke up my home. Told him I was a stranger in Houston. The girls gathered at the top of the stairs to see a fight. Seven of them. Six feet and an iron claw. That's bad on the nerves. (*breaks* L.) Kicked him in the mouth when he swung for my head with the claw. Would have lost an eye except for quick thinking. He rolled into the gutter and pulled a gun. Fired seven times. I was back upstairs. Left the place an hour later, dressed in silk and feathers, with a hat swung around over my face. Saw him standing on the corner, waiting. (*crossing* L.) Said, Care for a wiggle? Said he didn't. I went on down the street and left town. I don't suppose you ever had to put a dress on to save your skin, did you? (*crosses to* L. *of* C. *table and sits*)

JOE. (*signals NICK for beer*) No, and I never fell in love with a midget weighing thirty-nine pounds. Have another beer?

KIT CARSON. Thanks. Ever try to herd cattle on a bicycle? (*NICK crosses to* L. *of table* C. *with beer which KIT takes. NICK goes back to bar.*)

JOE. No. I never got around to that.

KIT CARSON. Left Houston with sixty cents in my pocket, gift of a girl named Lucinda. Walked fourteen miles in fourteen hours. Big house with barbed-wire all around, and big dogs. One thing I never could get around. Walked past the gate, anyway, from hunger and thirst. Dogs jumped up and came for me. Walked right into them, growing older every second. Went up to the door and knocked. Big negress opened the door, closed it quick. Said, On your way, white trash. Knocked again, Said, On your way. Again. On your way. Again. This time the old man himself opened the door, ninety, if he was a day. Sawed-off shotgun, too. Said, I ain't looking for trouble, Father. I'm hungry and thirsty, name's Cavanaugh. Took me in and made mint juleps for the two of us. Said, Living here alone, Father? Said, Drink and ask no questions. Maybe I am and maybe I ain't. You saw the lady. Draw your own conclusions. I'd heard of that, but didn't wink out of tact. If I told you that old Southern gentleman was my grandfather, you wouldn't believe me, would you?

JOE. I might.

KIT CARSON. Well, it so happens he wasn't. Would have been romantic if he had been, though.

JOE. Where did you herd cattle on a bicycle?

KIT CARSON. Toledo, Ohio, 1918.

JOE. Toledo, Ohio? They don't herd cattle in Toledo.

KIT CARSON. They don't anymore. They did in 1918. One fellow did, leastaways. Bookkeeper named Sam Gold. Straight from the East Side, New York. Sombrero, lariats, Bull Durham, two head of cattle and two bicycles. Called his place The Gold Bar Ranch, two acres, just outside the city limits. That was the year of the War, you'll remember.

JOE. Yeah, I remember, but how about herding them two cows on a bicycle? How'd you do it?

KIT CARSON. Easiest thing in the world. Rode no hands. Had to, otherwise couldn't lasso the cows. Worked for Sam Gold till the cows ran away. Bicycles scared them. They went into Toledo. Never saw hide nor hair of them again. Advertised in every paper, but never got them back. Broke his heart. Sold both bikes and returned to New York. Took four aces from a deck of red cards and walked to town. Poker. Fellow in the game named Chuck Collins, liked to gamble. Told him with a smile I didn't suppose he'd care to bet a hundred dollars I wouldn't hold four aces the next hand. Called it. My cards were red on the blank side. The other cards were blue. Plumb forgot all about it. Showed him four aces. Ace of spades, ace of clubs, ace of diamonds, ace of hearts. I'll remember them four cards if I live to be sixty. Would have been killed on the spot except for the hurricane that year.

Joe. Hurricane?

Kit Carson. You haven't forgotten the Toledo hurricane of 1918, have you?

Joe. No. There was no hurricane in Toledo in 1918, or any other year.

Kit Carson. For the love of God, then what do you suppose that commotion was? And how come I came to in Chicago dream-walking down State Street?

Joe. I guess they scared you.

Kit Carson. No, that wasn't it. You go back to the papers of November 1918, and I think you'll find there was a hurricane in Toledo. I remember sitting on the roof of a two-story house, floating northwest.

Joe. (*seriously*) Northwest?

Kit Carson. Now, son, don't tell me *you* don't believe me, either?

Joe. (*very seriously, energetically and sharply*) Of course I believe you. Living is an art. It's not bookkeeping. It takes a lot of rehearsing for a man to get to be himself.

Kit Carson. (*thoughtfully, smiling*) You're the first man I've ever met who believes me.

Joe. (*seriously*) Have another beer. (*TOM comes in* R. *with the Rand-McNally book, the revolver, and the box of cartridges.*)

JOE. (*to TOM*) Did you give her the toys?

TOM. Yeah, I gave them to her.

JOE. Did she stop crying?

TOM. No. She started crying harder than ever.

JOE. That's funny. I wonder why.

TOM. Joe, if I was a minute earlier, Frankie would have taken the bet and now we'd have about a thousand five hundred dollars. How much of it would you have given me, Joe?

JOE. If she'd marry you — *all* of it.

TOM. Would you, Joe?

JOE. (*opening packages, examining book first, and revolver next*) Sure. In this realm there's only one subject, and you're it. It's my duty to see that my subject is happy.

TOM. Joe, do you think we'll ever have eighty dollars for a race sometime again when there's a fifteen-to-one shot that we like, weather good, track fast, they get off to a good start, our horse doesn't get a call till the stretch, we think we're going to lose all that money, and then it wins, by a nose?

JOE. I didn't quite get that.

TOM. You know what I mean.

JOE. You mean the impossible. No, Tom, we won't. We were just a little late, that's all.

TOM. We might, Joe.

JOE. It's not likely.

TOM. Then how am I ever going to make enough money to marry her?

JOE. I don't know, Tom. Maybe you won't.

TOM. Joe, I got to marry Kitty. (*shaking his head*) You ought to see the crazy room she lives in.

JOE. What kind of room is it?

TOM. It's little. It crowds you in. It's bad, Joe. Kitty don't belong in a place like that.

JOE. You want to take her away from there?

TOM. Yeah. I want her to live in a house where there's room enough to live. Kitty ought to have a garden, or something.

JOE. You want to take care of her?

TOM. Yeah, sure, Joe. I ought to take care of somebody good that makes me feel like *I'm* somebody.

JOE. That means you'll have to get a job. What can you do?

TOM. I finished high school, but I don't know what I can do.

JOE. Sometimes when you think about it, what do you think you'd like to do?

TOM. Just sit around like you, Joe, and have somebody run errands for me and drink champagne and take things easy and never be broke and never worry about money.

(*WARN curtain*)

JOE. That's a noble ambition.

NICK. How do you do it?

JOE. I really don't know, but I think you've got to have the full co-operation of the Good Lord.

NICK. I can't understand the way you talk.

TOM. Joe, shall I go back and see if I can get her to stop crying?

JOE. Give me a hand and I'll go with you.

TOM. (*amazed*) What! You're going to get up already?

JOE. She's crying, isn't she?

TOM. She's crying. Worse than ever now.

JOE. I thought the toys would stop her.

TOM. I've seen you sit in one place from four in the morning till two the next morning.

JOE. At my best, Tom, I don't travel by foot. That's all. Come on. Give me a hand. I'll find some way to stop her from crying.

TOM. Joe, I never did tell you. You're a different kind of a guy.

JOE. Don't be silly. I don't understand things. I'm trying to understand them. (*TOM helps JOE up. He is a little drunk. They go out* R. *together. The telephone rings. DUDLEY jumps to his feet and runs to it.*)

CURTAIN

ACT THREE

*Room 21 of The New York Hotel, around the corner from
NICK's. This is set inside the main set. There is a bed
R.; a screen above bed; a door back of screen; a win-
dow in back of bed. A dresser is painted on the screen.
A small table above R. of bed. KITTY DUVAL, in a
dress she has carried around with her from the early
days in Ohio, is seated on the bed, tying a ribbon in
her hair. She looks at herself in the mirror. She is
deeply grieved at the change she sees in herself. She
stares at the bare, desolate walls of the room, looks
into the mirror again, takes off the ribbon, angry and
hurt. She lifts a book from the bed and tries to read.
She begins to sob again, takes an old picture of herself from foot of bed and looks at it, and sobs harder
than ever, falling on the bed and burying her face. She
turns over on the other side, as if even with her eyes
closed she cannot escape her sorrow. From one of the
other rooms of the hotel is coming the voice of a
YOUNG MAN singing "My Gal Sal." There is a
knock at the door.*

KITTY. (*sobbing*) Who is it?
TOM'S VOICE. Kitty, it's me. Tom. Me and Joe.

(*KITTY looks around the room, smiles at the remembrance of TOM, looks around the desolate room and
falls back sobbing. JOE, followed by TOM, comes in
quietly. JOE is holding a rather large toy carousel.
He takes the room in swiftly, amazed. He sets the toy
carousel on the floor, at the foot of KITTY's bed.*)

TOM. (*standing over KITTY and bending down close to her*) Don't cry any more, Kitty.

KITTY. (*not looking up, sobbing*) I don't like this life. (*JOE starts the carousel which makes a strange, sorrowful, tinkling music. The music begins slowly, becomes swift, gradually slows down, and ends. JOE himself is interested in the toy, watches and listens to it carefully.*)

TOM. Kitty. Joe got up from his chair at Nick's just to get you a toy and come here. This one makes music. We rode all over town in a cab to get it. Listen. (*KITTY sits up slowly, listening, while TOM watches her and JOE. Everything happens slowly and somberly. KITTY notices the photograph of herself when she was a little girl, lifts it, and looks at it again.*)

TOM. (*looking*) Who's that little girl, Kitty?

KITTY. That's me. When I was seven. (*hands the photo to TOM*)

TOM. Gee, you're pretty, Kitty. (*JOE reaches up for the photograph, which TOM hands to him. TOM returns to KITTY whom he finds as pretty now as she was at seven. JOE studies the photograph. KITTY looks up at TOM. There is no doubt that they really love one another. JOE looks up at them.*)

KITTY. Tom?

TOM. (*eagerly*) Yeah, Kitty.

KITTY. Tom, when you were a little boy what did you want to be?

TOM. (*a little bewildered, but eager to please her*) What, Kitty?

KITTY. Do you remember when you were a little a boy?

TOM. (*thoughtfully*) Yeah, I remember sometimes, Kitty.

KITTY. What did you want to be?

TOM. (*He looks at JOE. JOE holds TOM's eyes a moment. Then TOM is able to speak.*) Sometimes I wanted to be a locomotive engineer. Sometimes I wanted to be a policeman.

KITTY. I wanted to be a great actress (*She looks up into TOM's face*) Tom, didn't you ever want to be a doctor?

TOM. (*He looks at JOE. JOE hold's TOM's eyes again, encouraging TOM by his serious expression to go on talking.*) Yeah, now I remember. Sure, Kitty. I wanted to be a doctor — *once.*

KITTY. (*smiling sadly*) I'm so glad. Because I wanted to be an actress and have a young doctor come to the theater and see me and fall in love with me and send me flowers. (*JOE pantomimes to TOM, demanding that he go on talking*)

TOM. I would do that, Kitty.

KITTY. I wouldn't know who it was, and then one day I'd see him in the street and fall in love with him. I wouldn't know *he* was the one who was in love with me. I'd think about him all the time. I'd dream about him. I'd dream of being near him the rest of my life. I'd dream of having children that looked like him. I wouldn't be an actress all the time. Only until I found him and fell in love with him. After that we'd take a train and go to beautiful cities and see the wonderful people everywhere and give money to the poor and whenever people were sick he'd go to them and make them well again. (*TOM looks at JOE, bewildered, confused, and full of sorrow. KITTY is deep in memory, almost in a trance.*)

JOE. (*gently*) Talk to her, Tom. Be the wonderful young doctor she dreamed about and never found. Go ahead. Correct the errors of the world.

TOM. Joe. (*pathetically*) I don't know what to say.

(*There is rowdy singing in the hall. A loud young VOICE sings: "Sailing, sailing, over the bounding main."*)

VOICE. Kitty. Oh, Kitty! (*KITTY stirs, shocked, coming out of trance.*) Where the hell are you? Oh, Kitty. (*TOM jumps up, furiously.*)

WOMAN'S VOICE. (*in the hall*) Who you looking for, Sailor Boy?

VOICE. The most beautiful lay in the world.

WOMAN'S VOICE. Don't go any further.

VOICE. (*with impersonal contempt*) You? No. Not you. Kitty. You stink.

WOMAN'S VOICE. (*rasping, angry*) Don't you dare talk to me that way. You pickpocket.

VOICE. (*still impersonal, but louder*) Oh, I see. Want to get tough, hey? Close the door. Go hide.

WOMAN'S VOICE. You pickpocket. All of you. (*The door slams.*)

VOICE. (*roaring with laughter which is very sad*) Oh— Kitty. Room 21. Where the hell is that room?

TOM. (*to JOE*) Joe, I'll kill him.

KITTY. (*fully herself again, terribly frightened*) Who is it? (*She looks long and steadily at TOM and JOE. TOM is standing, excited and angry. JOE is completely at ease, his expression full of pity.*)

(*WARN Blackout*)

JOE. (*gently*) Tom. Just take him away.

VOICE. Here it is. Number 21. Three naturals. Heaven. My blue heaven. The west, a nest, and you. Molly and me. (*tragically*) Ah, to hell with everything. (*There is a loud knock at the door. KITTY turns away, as if seeking some place to be safe and protected. JOE doesn't even look toward the door. TOM opens the door. JOE turns and looks. In the doorway stands a young SAILOR—a good-looking boy of no more than twenty or so who is only drunk and lonely.*)

SAILOR. Hi-ya, Kitty. (*pause*) Oh. Visitors. Sorry. A thousand apologies. I'll come back later.

TOM. (*taking him by the shoulders, furiously*) If you do, I'll kill you. (*He pushes the frightened SAILOR away and closes the door.*)

JOE. Tom. You stay here with Kitty. I'm going down to Union Square to hire an automobile. I'll be back in a few minutes. We'll ride out to the ocean and watch the sun go down. Then we'll ride down the Great Highway to Half Moon Bay. We'll have supper down there, and you and Kitty can dance.

TOM. (*stupefied, unable to express his amazement and gratitude*) Joe, you mean you're going to go on an errand for *me*? You mean you're not going to send me?

JOE. That's right. (*He gestures toward KITTY, indicating that TOM shall talk to her, protect the innocence in her which is in so much danger when TOM isn't near, which TOM loves so deeply.*)

BLACKOUT

ACT FOUR

A little later.

NICK's again. *We are back to the time when TOM is helping JOE out of the place, on their way to KITTY's. They are almost off stage when the lights are on.*

WESLEY, the colored boy, is at the piano, playing the same song, — at the same place.

HARRY is on the little stage dancing.

WILLIE at marble-game.

NICK is behind the bar.

DUDLEY at table R.

The ARAB is in his place.

KIT CARSON is asleep on his folded arms.

DRUNK comes in R., *goes to the telephone for nickel that might be in the return chute. NICK goes to him. DRUNK shows money. Both cross to bar. NICK to back of bar, hands DRUNK a shot glass and bottle.)*

DRUNK. To the old, God bless them. (*another*) To the new, God love them. (*another*) To — children and small animals, like little dogs that don't bite. (*another, loudly*) To reforestation. (*searches for money, finds some*) To — President Taft. (*He goes out* R. *The telephone rings. KIT CARSON jumps up and starts to shadow box. DUDLEY runs to phone.*)

KIT CARSON. Come on, *all* of you, if you're looking for trouble. I never asked for quarter and I always gave it.

NICK. (*reproachfully*) Hey, Kit Carson.

DUDLEY. (*on the phone.*) Hello. Who? Nick. Yes. He's here. (*to NICK*) It's for you. I think it's important.

NICK. (*crossing up to the phone*) Important! *What's* important?

DUDLEY. He sounded like big-shot.

NICK. Big *what*? (*to WESLEY and HARRY*) Hey, you. Quiet. I want to hear this important stuff. (*WESLEY stops playing the piano. HARRY stops dancing. KIT CARSON comes close to R. of NICK.*)

KIT CARSON. If there's anything I can do, name it. I'll do it for you. I'm fifty-eight years old; been through three wars; married four times; the father of countless children whose *names* I don't even know. I've got no money. I live from hand to mouth. But if there's anything I can do, name it. I'll do it.

NICK. Listen, Pop. For a moment, please sit down and go back to sleep — *for me.*

KIT CARSON. (*crossing to L. of C. table*) I can do that, too. (*He sits down, folds his arms, and puts his head into them, but not for long. As NICK begins to talk, he listens carefully, gets to his feet, and then begins to express in pantomime the moods of each of NICK's remarks.*)

NICK. (*on phone*) Yeah? (*pause*) Who? Oh, I see. (*listens*) Why don't you leave them alone? (*listens*) The church-people? Well, to hell with the church-people. I'm a Catholic myself. (*listens*) All right. I'll send them away. I'll tell them to lay low for a couple of days. Yeah, I know how it is. (*He is about to hand up. NICK's daughter ANNA comes in R. shyly, looking at her father, and stands unnoticed by the piano.*) What? (*very angry*) Listen. I don't like that Blick. He was here this morning, and I told him not to come back. I'll keep the girls out of here. You keep Blick out of here. (*listens*) I know his brother-in-law is important, but I don't want him to come down here. He looks for trouble everywhere, and he always finds it. I don't break any laws. I've got a dive in the lousiest part of town. Five years nobody's been robbed, murdered, or gypped. I leave people alone. Your swanky joints uptown make trouble for you every night. (*NICK gestures to WESLEY — keeps listening on the phone — puts his hand over the mouth-piece. To WESLEY and HARRY:*) Start playing again. My ears have got a headache. Go into your dance, son. (*WESLEY begins to play again. HARRY begins to dance. NICK, into mouthpiece:*) Yeah. I'll keep them out. Just see that Blick doesn't come around and start something. O.K. (*He hangs up, crosses up c.*)

KIT CARSON. (*following to l. of NICK*) Trouble coming?

NICK. That lousy Vice Squad again. It's that gorilla Blick.

KIT CARSON. Anybody at all. You can count on me. What kind of gorilla is this gorilla Blick?

NICK. Very dignified. Toenails on his fingers.

ANNA. (*to KIT CARSON, with great, warm, beautiful pride, pointing at NICK*) That's my father.

KIT CARSON. (*leaping with amazement at the beautiful voice, the wondrous face, the magnificent event*) Well, bless your heart, child. Bless your lovely heart. I had a little daughter point me out in a crowd once.

NICK. (*surprised*) Anna. What the hell are you doing here? Get back home where you belong and help Grandma cook me some supper. (*ANNA smiles at her father, understanding him, knowing that his words are words of love. She turns and goes r., looking at him all the way out, as much as to say that she would be cook for him the rest of her life. NICK stares at the swinging doors. KIT CARSON moves toward them, two or three steps. ANNA pushes open one of the doors and peeks in, to look at her father again. She waves to him, turns and runs. NICK is very sad. He doesn't know what to do. He gets a glass and a bottle, pours himself a drink, swallows some.*)

It isn't enough, so he pours more and swallows the whole drink. To himself:) My beautiful, beautiful baby. Anna, she is you again. (*He brings out a handkerchief, touches his eyes, and blows his nose. KIT CARSON moves close to NICK, watching NICK's face. NICK looks at him. Loudly, almost making KIT jump:)* You're broke, aren't you?

KIT CARSON. Always. *Always.*

NICK. All right. Go into the kitchen and give Sam a hand. Eat some food and when you come back you can have a couple of beers.

KIT CARSON. (*studying NICK*) Anything at all. I know a good man when I see one. (*He goes out back c.*)

(*ELSIE MANDELSPIEGEL comes in R. She is a beautiful, dark girl, with a sorrowful, wise, dreaming face, almost on the verge of tears, and full of pity. There is an aura of dream about her. She moves softly and gently, as if everything around her were unreal and pathetic. DUDLEY doesn't notice her for a moment or two. When he does finally see her, he is so amazed, he can barely move or speak. Her presence has the effect of changing him completely. He gets up from his chair, as if in a trance, and walks toward her, smiling sadly.*)

ELSIE. (*crossing to chair R. of c. table*) Hello, Dudley.

DUDLEY. Elsie.

ELSIE. (*sits*) I'm sorry. So many people are sick. Last night a little boy died. I love you, but—

DUDLEY. (crossing to chair L. of c. table) Elsie. You'll never know how glad I am to see you. (*sits*) Just to *see* you. I was afraid I'd never see you again. It was driving me crazy. I didn't want to live. Honest. (*The KILLER and her SIDEKICK come in R. and go to bar.*) I know.

You told me before, but I can't help it, Elsie. I love you.

ELSIE. I know you love me, and I love you, but don't you see love is impossible in this world?

DUDLEY. Maybe it isn't, Elsie.

ELSIE. Love is for the birds. They have wings to fly away on when it's time for flying. For tigers in the jungle because they don't know their end. We know *our* end. Every night I watch over poor, dying men. I hear them breathing, crying, talking in their sleep. Crying for air and water and love, for mother and field and sunlight. *We* can never know love or greatness. We *should* know both.

DUDLEY. Elsie, I love you.

ELSIE. You want to live. *I* want to live, too, but where? Where can we escape our poor world?

DUDLEY. Elsie, we'll find a place.

ELSIE. All right. We'll try again. We'll go together to a room in a cheap hotel, and dream that the world is beautiful, and that living is full of love and greatness. But in the morning, can we forget debts, and duties, and the cost of ridiculous things?

DUDLEY. Sure, we can, Elsie.

ELSIE. All right, Dudley. Of course. (*rises*) Come on. The time for the new pathetic war has come. Let's hurry, before they dress you, stand you in line, hand you a gun, and have you kill and be killed. (*She leads him out* R.)

KILLER. Nick, what the hell kind of a joint are you running?

NICK. Well, it's not out of the world. It's on a street in a city, and people come and go. They bring whatever they've got with them and they say what they must say.

THE OTHER STREETWALKER. It's floozies like her that raise hell with our racket.

NICK. Oh, yeah. Finnegan telephoned.

THE OTHER STREETWALKER. What the hell does *he* want?

NICK. Spend your time at the movies for the next couple of days.

KILLER. They're all lousy. (*mincing and smoking*) All about love.

NICK. Lousy or not lousy, for a couple of days the flat-foots are going to be romancing you, so stay out of here, and lay low.

KILLER. I always was a pushover for a man in uniform, with badge, a club and a gun. (*KRUPP comes in* R. *The girls put down their drinks.*)

NICK. O.K., get going. (*The girls begin to leave and meet KRUPP, who pauses to look them over.*)

THE OTHER STREETWALKER. We was just going.

KILLER. We was formerly models at Magnin's. (*They go out* R.)

KRUPP. (*at the bar*) The strike isn't enough, so they've got to put us on the tails of the girls, too. I don't know. I wish to God I was back in the Sunset holding the hands of kids going home from school, where I belong. I don't like trouble. Give me a beer. (*NICK gives him a beer. He drinks some.*) Right now, McCarthy, my best friend, is with sixty strikers who want to stop the finks who are going to try to unload the *Mary Luckenbach* tonight. Why the hell McCarthy ever became a longshoreman instead of a professor of some kind is something I'll never know.

NICK. Cowboys and Indians, cops and robbers, longshoremen and finks.

KRUPP. They're all guys who are trying to be happy; trying to make a living; support a family; bring up children; enjoy sleep. Go to a movie; take a drive on Sunday. They're all good guys, so out of nowhere, comes trouble.

All they want is a chance to get out of debt and relax in front of a radio while Amos and Andy go through their act. What the hell do they always want to make trouble for? I been thinking everything over, Nick, and you know what I think?

NICK. No. What?

KRUPP. I think we're all crazy. It came to me while I was on my way to Pier 27. All of a sudden it hit me like a ton of bricks. A thing like that never happened to me before. Here we are in this wonderful world, full of all the wonderful things — here we are — all of us, and look at us. Just look at us. We're crazy. We're nuts. We've got everything, but we always feel lousy and dissatisfied just the same.

NICK. Of course we're crazy. Even so, we've got to go on living together.

KRUPP. There's no hope. I don't suppose it's right for an officer of the law to feel the way I feel, but, by God, right or not right, that's how I feel. Why are we all so lousy? This is a good world. It's wonderful to get up in the morning and go out for a little walk and smell the trees and see the streets and the kids going to school and the clouds in the sky. It's wonderful just to be able to move around and whistle a song if you feel like it, or maybe try to sing one. This is a nice world. So why do they make all the trouble?

NICK. I don't know. Why?

KRUPP. We're crazy, that's why. We're no good any more. All the corruption everywhere. The poor kids selling themselves. A couple of years ago they were in grammar school. Everybody trying to get a lot of money in a hurry. Everybody betting the horses. Nobody going quietly for a little walk to the ocean. Nobody taking things easy and not wanting to make some kind of a killing. Nick, I'm going to quit being a cop. Let somebody else keep law and order. The stuff I hear about at headquarters. I'm thirty-seven years old, and I still can't get used to it. The only trouble is, the wife'll raise hell.

NICK. Ah, the wife.

KRUPP. She's a wonderful woman, Nick. We've got two of the swellest boys in the world. Twelve and seven years old.

NICK. I didn't know that. (*ARAB, WESLEY and WILLIE listen to KRUPP.*)

KRUPP. Sure. But what'll I do? I've wanted to quit for seven years. I wanted to quit the day they began putting me through the school. I didn't quit. What'll I do if I quit? Where's money going to be coming in from?

NICK. That's one of the reasons we're all crazy. We don't know where it's going to be coming in from, except from wherever it happens to be coming in from at the time, which we don't usually like. (*ARAB, WESLEY and WILLIE go back to former interests.*)

KRUPP. Every once in a while I catch myself being mean, hating people just because they're down and out, broke and hungry, sick or drunk. And then when I'm with the stuffed shirts at headquarters, all of a sudden I'm nice to them, trying to make an impression. On who? People I don't like. And I feel disgusted. (*with finality*) I'm going to quit. That's all. Quit. Out. I'm going to give them back the uniform and the gadgets that go with it. I don't want any part of it. (*takes off badge and slams it on bar*) This is a good world. What do they want to make all the trouble for all the time?

ARAB. No foundation. All the way down the line.

KRUPP. What?

ARAB. No foundation. No foundation.

KRUPP. I'll say there's no foundation.

ARAB. All the way down the line.

KRUPP. (*to NICK*) Is that all he ever says?

NICK. That's all he's been saying *this* week.

KRUPP. What is he, anyway?

NICK. He's an Arab, or something like that.

KRUPP. No, I mean what's he do for a living?

NICK. (*to ARAB*) What do you do for a living, brother?

ARAB. Work. Work all my life. All my life, work. From small boy to old man, work. In old country, work. In new country, work. In New York. Pittsburgh. Detroit. Chicago. Imperial Valley. San Francisco. Work. No beg. Work. For what? Nothing. Three boys in old country. Twenty years, not see. Lost. Dead. Who knows? What. What-not. No foundation. All the way down the line.

KRUPP. What'd he say last week?

NICK. Didn't say anything. Played the harmonica.

ARAB. Old country song, I play. (*He brings a harmonica from his back pocket and begins to play an old country song.*)

KRUPP. Seems like a nice guy.

NICK. Nicest guy in the world.

KRUPP. (*bitterly*) But crazy. Just like all the rest of us. Stark raving mad. (*WESLEY and HARRY long ago stopped playing and dancing. They sat at L.C. table together and talked for a while; then began playing casino or rummy. When the ARAB begins his solo on the harmonica, they stop their game to listen.*)

WESLEY. You hear that?

(*WARN curtain*)

HARRY. That's *something*.

WESLEY. That's crying. That's crying.

HARRY. I want to make people laugh.

WESLEY. That's deep, deep crying. That's crying a long time ago. That's crying a thousand years ago. Some place five thousand miles away.

HARRY. Do you think you can play to that?

WESLEY. I want to *sing* to that, but I can't *sing.*

HARRY. You try and play to that. I'll try to dance. (*WESLEY goes to the piano, and after closer listening, he begins to accompany the harmonica solo. HARRY goes to the little stage and after a few efforts begins to dance to the song. This keeps up quietly for some time. KRUPP and NICK have been silent, KRUPP drinking a beer; NICK fooling around behind the bar.*)

KRUPP. Well, anyhow, Nick. (*picks up badge and puts it on*)

NICK. Hmmmmmmmm?

KRUPP. What I said. Forget it.

NICK. Sure.

KRUPP. It gets me down once in a while.

NICK. No harm in talking.

KRUPP. Keep the girls out of here. (*He starts for door* R. *HARRY starts double time whirl.*)

NICK. Take it easy.

CURTAIN

ACT FIVE

NICK's. That evening. Fog-horns are heard throughout this scene. A GENTLEMAN in evening clothes and a top hat, and his LADY, also in evening clothes, are entering R. WILLIE, the marble-game maniac, is still at the marble game. NICK is behind the bar. JOE is at table C., looking at the book of maps of the countries of Europe. The box containing the revolver and the box containing cartridges are on the table, beside his glass. He is at peace, his hat tilted back on his head, a calm expression on his face. TOM is leaning against the bar, dreaming of love and KITTY. The ARAB is gone. WESLEY and HARRY, the comedian, are gone for the moment. KIT CARSON is watching the boy play the marble game. The MAN and LADY take L.C. table. She sits R. of it, he L. NICK gives them a menu.

Outside, in the street, the Salvation Army people are playing a song. Big drum, cornet, big horn, and tambourine. They are singing too. "The Blood of the Lamb." The music and words come into the place faintly and comically. This is followed by an old sinner testifying, it's the DRUNK. All his words are not intelligible, but his message is unmistakable. He is saved. He wants to sin no more. And so on.

LADY. Oh, come on, please. (*The GENTLEMAN follows miserably.*)

DRUNK. (*testifying, unmistakably drunk*) Brothers and sisters. I was a sinner. I chewed tobacco and chased women. Oh, I sinned, brothers and sisters. And then I was saved. Saved by the Salvation Army, God forgive me.

97

JOE. Let's see now. Here's a city. Pribor. Czecho-slo-vakia. Little, lovely, lonely Czecho-slovakia. I wonder what kind of a place Pribor was? (*calling*) Pribor! *Pribor*! (*TOM leaps.*)

LADY. What's the matter with him?

MAN. Drunk.

TOM. Who you calling, Joe?

JOE. Pribor.

TOM. Who's Pribor?

JOE. He's a Czech. And a Slav. A Czecho-slovakian.

LADY. How interesting.

MAN. He's drunk.

JOE. Tom, Pribor's a city in Czecho-slovakia.

TOM. Oh. (*pause*) You sure were nice to her, Joe.

JOE. Kitty Duval? She's one of the finest people in the world.

TOM. It sure was nice of you to hire an automobile and take us for a drive along the ocean-front and down to Half Moon Bay.

JOE. Those three hours were the most delightful, the most somber, and the most beautiful I have ever known.

TOM. Why, Joe?

JOE. Why? I'm a student. (*lifting his voice*) Tom. (*TOM crosses below and sits* L. *of table* C. *Quietly:*) I'm a student. I study all things. All. All. And when my study reveals something of beauty in a place or in a person where by all rights only ugliness or death should be revealed, then I know how full of goodness this life is. And that's a good thing to know. That's a truth I shall always seek to verify.

LADY. Are you *sure* he's drunk?

MAN. He's either drunk, or just naturally crazy.

TOM. Joe?

JOE. Yeah.

Tom. You won't get sore or anything?

Joe. What is it, Tom?

Tom. Joe, where do you get all that money? You paid for the automobile. You paid for supper and the two bottles of champagne at the Half Moon Bay Restaurant. You moved Kitty out of the New York Hotel around the corner to the St. Francis Hotel on Powell Street. I saw you pay her rent. I saw you give her money for new clothes. Where do you get all that money, Joe? Three years now and I've never asked.

Joe. (*He gestures the question aside impatiently. He smiles with some inner thought and suddenly lifts the box containing the gun, and the other with the cartridges. Looking at TOM sorrowfully, a little irritated, not so much with TOM as with the world and himself, his own superiority. He speaks clearly, slowly, and solemnly.*) Now don't be a fool, Tom. Listen carefully. If anybody's got any money — to hoard or to throw away — you can be sure he stole it from other people. Not from rich people who can spare it, but from poor people who can't. From their lives and from their dreams. I'm no exception. I *earned* the money I throw away. I stole it like everybody else does. I hurt people to get it. Loafing around this way, I *still* earn money. The money itself earns *more.* I *still* hurt people. I don't know who they are, or where they are. If I did, I'd feel worse than I do. I've got a Christian conscience in a world that's got no conscience at all. The world's trying to get some sort of a *social* conscience, but it's having a devil of a time trying to do *that.* I've got money. I'll always have money, as long as this world stays the way it is. I don't work. I don't make anything. (*He sips.*) I drink. I worked when I was a kid. I worked *hard.* I mean hard, Tom. People are supposed to enjoy living. I got tired. (*He lifts the gun and looks at it while he talks.*) I decided to get even on the world. Well, you can't enjoy living unless you work. Unless you do something. I don't do anything. I don't *want* to do anything any more. There isn't anything I can do that won't make me feel embarrassed. Because I can't do simple, good things. I haven't the patience. And I'm too smart. Money is the guiltiest thing in the world. It stinks. Now, don't ever bother me about it again.

TOM. I didn't mean to make you feel bad, Joe.

JOE. (*slowly*) Here. Take this gun out in the street and give it to some worthy hold-up man.

LADY. What's he saying?

MAN. (*uncrosses legs*) You wanted to visit a honky-tonk. Well, *this* is a honky-tonk. (*to the world*) Married twenty-eight years and she's still looking for adventure.

TOM. How should I know who's a hold-up man?

JOE. Take it away. Give it to somebody.

TOM. (*bewildered*) Do I *have* to *give* it to somebody?

JOE. Of course.

TOM. Can't I take it back and get some of our money?

JOE. Don't talk like a business man. Look around and find somebody who appears to be in need of a gun and give it to him. It's a good gun, isn't it?

TOM. The man said it was, but how can I tell who needs a gun?

JOE. Tom, you've seen good people who needed guns, haven't you?

TOM. I don't remember. Joe, I might give it to the wrong kind of guy. He might do something crazy.

JOE. All right. I'll find somebody myself. (*TOM rises.*) Here's some money. Go get me this week's *Life, Liberty, Time,* and six or seven packages of chewing gum.

TOM. (*swiftly, in order to remember each item*) *Life, Liberty, Time,* and six or seven packages of chewing gum?

JOE. That's right.

TOM. All that chewing gum? What kind?

JOE. Any kind. Mix 'em up. All kinds.

TOM. Licorice, too?

JOE. Licorice, by all means.

TOM. Juicy Fruit?

JOE. Juicy Fruit.

TOM. Tutti-frutti?

JOE. Is there such a gum?

TOM. I think so.

JOE. All right. Tutti-frutti, too. Get *all* the kinds. Get as many kinds as they're selling.

TOM. *Life, Liberty, Time,* and all the different kinds of gum. (*He begins to go* R.)

JOE. (*calling after him loudly*) Get some jelly beans too. All the different colors.

TOM. All right, Joe.

JOE. And the longest panatela cigar you can find. Six of them.

TOM. Panatela. I got it.

JOE. Give a news-kid a dollar.

TOM. O.K., Joe.

JOE. Give some old man a dollar.

TOM. O.K., Joe.

JOE. Give them Salvation Army people in the street a couple of dollars and ask them to sing that song that goes — (*He sings loudly.*) Let the lower lights be burning, send a gleam across the wave.

TOM. (*swiftly*) Let the lower lights be burning, send a gleam across the wave.

JOE. That's it. (*He goes on with the song, very loudly and religiously.*) Some poor, dying, struggling seaman, you may rescue, you may save. (*halts*)

TOM. O.K., Joe. I got it. *Life, Liberty, Time,* all the kinds of gum they're selling, jelly beans, six panatela cigars, a dollar for a news-kid, a dollar for an old man, two dollars for the Salvation Army. Let the lower lights be burning, send a gleam across the wave.

JOE. That's it. (*TOM goes out* R.)

LADY. He's absolutely insane.

MAN. (*wearily*) You asked me to take you to a honky-tonk, instead of to the Mark Hopkins. You're *here* in a honky-tonk. I can't help it if he's crazy. Do you want to go back to where people *aren't* crazy?

LADY. No, not just yet.

MAN. Well, all right then. Don't be telling me every minute that he's crazy.

LADY. You needn't be huffy about it. (*MAN refuses to answer. When JOE began to sing, KIT CARSON turned away from the marble-game and listened. While the MAN and LADY are arguing he comes over to JOE's table.*)

KIT CARSON. Presbyterian?

JOE. I attended a Presbyterian Sunday School.

KIT CARSON. Fond of singing?

JOE. On occasion. Have a drink?

KIT CARSON. Thanks.

JOE. Get a glass and sit down. (*KIT CARSON gets a glass from NICK, returns to the table, sits down, JOE pours him a drink, they touch glasses just as the Salvation Army people begin to fulfill the request. They sip some champagne, and at the proper moment begin to sing the song together, sipping champagne, raising hell with the tune, swinging it, and so on.*) Always was fond of that song. Used to sing it at the top of my voice. Never saved a seaman in my life.

KIT CARSON. I saved a seaman once. Well, he wasn't exactly a seaman. He was a darky named Wellington. Heavy-set sort of a fellow. Nice personality, but no friends to speak of. Not until I came along, at any rate. In New Orleans. In the summer of the year 1899. No. Ninety-eight. I was a lot younger of course, and had no mustache, but was regarded by many people as a man of means.

JOE. Know anything about guns?

KIT CARSON. All there is to know. Didn't fight the Ojibways for nothing. Up there in the Lake Takalooca Country, in Michigan. (*remembering*) Along about in 1881 or two. Fought 'em right up to the shore of the Lake. Made 'em swim for Canada. One fellow in particular, an Indian named Harry Daisy.

JOE. (*opening the box containing the revolver*) What sort of a gun would you say this is? Any good?

KIT CARSON. (*At sight of gun, he is scared to death.*) Yep. That looks like a pretty nice hunk of shooting iron. That's a six-shooter. Shot a man with a six-shooter once. Got him through the palm of his right hand. Lifted his arm to wave to a friend. Thought it was a bird. Fellow named, I believe, Carroway. Larrimore Carroway.

JOE. Know how to work one of these things? (*He offers KIT CARSON the revolver, which is old and enormous.*)

KIT CARSON. (*laughing at the absurd question*) Know how to work it? Hand me that little gun, son, and I'll show you all about it. (*JOE hands KIT the revolver. Obviously bluffing:*) Let's see now. This is probably a new kind of six-shooter. After my time. Haven't nicked an Indian in years. I believe this here place is supposed to move out. (*He fools around and gets the barrel out for loading.*) That's it. There it is.

JOE. Look all right?

KIT CARSON. It's a good gun. You've got a good gun there, son. I'll explain it to you. You see these holes? Well, that's where you put the cartridges.

JOE. (*taking some cartridges out of the box*) Here. Show me how it's done.

KIT CARSON. (*scared to death but bluffing beautifully*) Well, son, you take 'em one by one and put 'em in the holes, like this. There's one. Two. Three. Four. Five. Six. Then you get the barrel back in place. Then cock it. Then all you do is aim and fire. (*He points the gun at the LADY. The gun is loaded, but uncocked.*)

JOE. It's all set?

KIT CARSON. Ready to kill.

JOE. Let me hold it. (*KIT hands JOE the gun. The LADY and MAN are scared to death. LADY rises.*)

KIT CARSON. Careful, now, son. Don't cock it. Many a man's lost an eye fooling with a loaded gun. Fellow I used to know named Danny Donovan lost a nose. Ruined his whole life. (*LADY sits.*) Hold it firm. Squeeze the trigger. Don't snap it. Spoils your aim.

JOE. Thanks. Let's see if I can unload it. (*He begins to unload it.*)

KIT CARSON. Of course you can. (*JOE unloads the revolver, looks at it very closely, puts the cartridges back into the box and puts them away in his overcoat pocket.*)

JOE. (*looking at gun*) I'm mighty grateful to you. Always wanted to see one of those things close up. Is it really a good one?

KIT CARSON. It's a beaut, son.

JOE. (*aims the empty gun at a bottle on the bar*) Bang! (*grinding of marble game*)

WILLIE. (*at the marble game*) Oh, Boy! (*loudly, triumphantly*) There you are, Nick. Thought I couldn't do it, hey? *Now,* watch. (*The machine begins to make a special kind of noise. Lights go on and off, some red, some green. A bell rings loudly six times.*) One. Two. Three. Four. Five. Six. (*An American flag jumps up.*

WILLIE comes to attention, salutes.) Oh, boy, what a beautiful country. (*A music-box version of the song* "America." *Singing:*) My country, 'tis of thee, sweet land of liberty, of thee I sing. (*Everything quiets down. The flag goes back into the machine. WILLIE is thrilled, amazed, delighted. Everybody has watched the performance of the defeated machine from wherever he happened to be when the performance began. WILLIE, looking around at everybody, as if they had all been on the side of the machine.*) O.K. How's that? I knew I could do it. (*to NICK*) Six nickels. (*NICK hands him six nickels. WILLIE goes over to JOE and KIT. Exuberantly, pointing a finger, gesturing wildly:*) Took me a little while, but I finally did it. It's scientific, really. With a little skill a man can make a modest living beating the marble-games. Not that that's what I want to do. I just don't like the idea of anything getting the best of me. A machine or anything else. (*doubling his fist*) Myself, I'm the kind of guy who makes up his mind to do something, and then goes to work and does it. There's no other way a man can be a success at anything. (*indicating the letter "F" on his sweater*) See that letter? That don't stand for some little-bitty high school somewhere. That stands for *me.* Faroughli. Willie Faroughli. I'm an Assyrian. We've got a civilization six or seven centuries old, I think. Somewhere along in there. Ever hear of Osman? Harold Osman? He's an Assyrian, too. He's got an orchestra down in Fresno. (*He goes to the LADY and MAN.*) I've never seen you before in my life, but I can tell from the clothes you wear and the company you keep (*graciously indicating the LADY*) that you're a man who looks every problem straight in the eye, and then goes to work and solves it. (*He bangs his fist into his left palm violently.*) I'm that way myself. (*three swift, ferocious bangs*) Well.

(*He smiles beautifully.*) It's been wonderful talking to a nicer type of people for a change. Well. I'll be seeing you. So long. (*He turns, takes two steps, returns to the table. Very politely and seriously:*) Good-by, lady. You've got a good man there. Take good care of him. (*WILLIE exits* R., *saluting JOE and the world. NICK goes into the kitchen, rear* C.)

KIT CARSON. (*to JOE*) By God, for a while there I didn't think that young Assyrian was going to do it. That fellow's got something. (*TOM comes back* R. *with the magazines and other stuff.*)

JOE. Get it all?

TOM. Yeah. I had a little trouble finding the jelly beans.

JOE. Let's take a look at them.

TOM. These are the jelly beans. (*JOE puts his hand into the cellophane bag and takes out a handful of the jelly beans, looks at them, smiles, and tosses a couple into his mouth.*)

JOE. Same as ever. Have some. (*He offers the bag to KIT.*)

KIT CARSON. (*flirting*) Thanks! I remember the first time I ever ate jelly beans. I was six, or at the most seven. Must have been in (*slowly*) eighteen — seventy-seven. Seven or eight. Baltimore.

JOE. Have some, Tom.

TOM. (*takes some*) Thanks, Joe.

JOE. Let's have some of that chewing gum. (*He dumps all the packages of gum out of the bag onto the table.*)

KIT CARSON. (*flirting*) Me and a boy named Clark. Quinton Clark. Became a Senator.

JOE. Yeah. Tutti-frutti, all right. (*He opens a package and folds all five pieces into his mouth.*) Always wanted to see how many I could chew at one time. Tell you what, Tom. I'll bet I can chew more at one time than you can.

TOM. (*delighted*) All right. (*They both begin to fold gum into their mouths.*)

KIT CARSON. I'll referee. Now, one at a time. How many you got?

JOE. Six.

KIT CARSON. All right. Let Tom catch up with you.

JOE. (*while TOM's catching up*) Did you give a dollar to a news-kid?

TOM. Yeah, sure.

JOE. What'd he say?

TOM. Thanks.

JOE. What sort of a kid was he?

TOM. Little, dark kid. I guess he's Italian.

JOE. Did he seem pleased?

TOM. Yeah.

JOE. That's good. Did you give a dollar to an old man?

TOM. Yeah.

JOE. Was he pleased?

TOM. Yeah.

JOE. Good. How many you got in your mouth?

TOM. Six.

JOE. All right. I got six, too. (*He folds one more in his mouth. TOM folds one too*)

KIT CARSON. Seven. Seven each. (*They each fold one more into their mouths, very solemnly, chewing them into the main hunk of gum.*) Eight. Nine. Ten.

JOE. (*delighted*) Always wanted to do this. (*He picks up one of the magazines.*) Let's see what's going on in the world. (*He turns the pages and keeps folding gum into his mouth and chewing.*)

KIT CARSON. Eleven. Twelve. (*KIT continues to count while JOE and TOM continue the contest. In spite of what they are doing, each is very serious.*)

TOM. Joe, what'd you want to move Kitty into the St. Francis Hotel for?

JOE. She's a better woman than any of them tramp society dames that hang around that lobby.

TOM. Yeah, but do you think she'll feel at home up there?

JOE. Maybe not at first, but after a couple of days she'll be all right. A nice big room. A bed for sleeping in. Good clothes. Good food. She'll be all right, Tom.

TOM. I hope so. Don't you think she'll get lonely up there with nobody to talk to?

JOE. (*looking at TOM sharply, almost with admiration, pleased but severe*) There's nobody *anywhere* for *her* to talk to—except *you.*

TOM. (*amazed and delighted*) *Me,* Joe?

JOE. (*While TOM and KIT CARSON listen carefully, KIT with great appreciation:*) Yes, you. By the grace of God, you're the other half of that girl. Not the angry woman that swaggers into this waterfront dive and shouts because the world has kicked her around. *Anybody* can have *her.* You belong to the little kid in Ohio who once dreamed of living. Not with her carcass, for *money,* so she can have food and clothes, and pay rent. With *all* of her. *I* put her in that hotel, so she can have a chance to gather herself together again. She can't do that in the New York Hotel. You saw what happened there. There's nobody anywhere for her to talk to, except you. They all make her talk like a whore. After a while, she'll *believe* them. Then she won't be able to remember. She'll get lonely. Sure. People can get lonely for *misery,* even. I want her to go on being lonely for *you,* so she can come together again the way she was meant to be from the beginning. Loneliness is good for people. Right now it's the only thing for Kitty. Any more licorice?

TOM. (*dazed*) What? Licorice? (*looking around busily*) I guess we've chewed all the licorice in. We still got Clove,

Peppermint, Doublemint, Beechnut, Teaberry, and Juicy Fruit.

JOE. Licorice used to be my favorite. Don't worry about her, Tom, she'll be all right. You really want to marry her, don't you?

TOM. (*nodding*) Honest to God, Joe. (*pathetically*) Only, I haven't got any money.

JOE. Couldn't you be a prize-fighter or something like that?

TOM. Naaaah. I couldn't hit a man if I wasn't sore at him. He'd have to do something that made me hate him.

JOE. You've got to figure out something to do that you won't mind doing very much.

TOM. I wish I could, Joe.

JOE. (*thinking deeply, suddenly*) Tom, would you be embarrassed driving a truck?

TOM. (*hit by a thunderbolt*) Joe, I never thought of that. I'd like that. Travel. Highways. Little towns. Coffee and hot cakes. Beautiful valleys and mountains and streams and trees and daybreak and sunset.

JOE. There *is* poetry in it, at that.

TOM. Joe, that's just the kind of work I *should* do. Just sit there and travel, and look, and smile, and bust out laughing. Could Kitty go with me, sometimes?

JOE. I don't know. Get me the phone book. Can you drive a truck?

TOM. (*crossing to phone*) Joe, you know I can drive a truck, or any kind of thing with a motor and wheels. (*TOM takes JOE the phone book. JOE turns the pages.*)

JOE. (*looking*) Here! Here it is. Tuxedo 7900. Here's a nickel. Get me that number. (*TOM goes to telephone, dials the number.*)

TOM. Hello.

JOE. Ask for Mr. Keith.

TOM. I'd like to talk to Mr. Keith. (*pause*) Mr. Keith.

JOE. Take that gum out of your mouth for a minute.

TOM. (*removes the gum*) Mr. Keith. Yeah. That's right. Hello, Mr. Keith?

JOE. Tell him to hold the line.

TOM. Hold the line, please.

JOE. Give me a hand, Tom. (*TOM helps JOE to the telephone. At phone, wad of gum in fingers delicately:*) Keith? Joe. Yeah. Fine. Forget it. (*pause*) Have you got a place for a good driver? (*pause*) I don't think so. (*to TOM*) You haven't got a driver's license, have you?

TOM. (*worried*) No. But I can get one, Joe.

JOE. (*at phone*) No, but he can get one easy enough. To hell with the union. He'll join later. All right, call him a Vice-President and say he drives for relaxation. Sure. What do you mean? Tonight? I don't know why not. San Diego? All right, let him start driving without a license. What the hell's the difference? Yeah. Sure. Look him over. Yeah. I'll send him right over. Right. (*He hangs up.*) Thanks. (*to telephone*)

TOM. (*helping JOE back to his seat*) Am I going to get the job?

JOE. (*sits*) He wants to take a look at you.

TOM. (*breaks to* R.) Do I look all right, Joe?

JOE. (*looking at him carefully*) Hold up your head. Stick out your chest. How do you feel?

TOM. (*does these things*) Fine.

JOE. You *look* fine, too. (*KIT CARSON has now reached twenty-seven sticks each. JOE takes his wad of gum out of his mouth and wraps* Liberty *magazine around it.*)

JOE. You win, Tom. Now, look. (*He bites off the tip of a very long panatela cigar, lights it, and hands one to TOM, and another to KIT.*) Have yourselves a pleasant

smoke. Here. (*He hands two more to TOM.*) Give those
slummers one each. (*He indicates the LADY and MAN.
TOM goes over and without a word gives a cigar each to
the MAN and the LADY then crosses below to* R. *of JOE.
At first they are a little offended; then the MAN lights his
cigar. The LADY looks at the cigar a moment, then bites
off the tip the way JOE did.*)

MAN. What do you think you're doing?

LADY. Really, dear. I'd like to.

MAN. Oh, this is too much.

LADY. I'd *really,* really like to, dear. (*turns to KIT, who
rises and crosses to* R. *of LADY*)

MAN. (*loudly*) The mother of five grown men, and
she's still looking for *romance.* (*The LADY timidly
scratches a match, puts the cigar in her mouth, KIT lights
it for her, and she begins to smoke, feeling wonderful.*)
No, I forbid it.

JOE. (*shouting*) What's the matter with you? Why
don't you leave her alone? What are you always pushing
your women around for? (*almost without a pause*) Now,
look, Tom. Here's ten bucks.

TOM. Ten bucks?

JOE. He may want you to get into a truck and begin
driving to San Diego tonight.

TOM. Joe, I got to tell Kitty.

JOE. I'll tell her.

TOM. Joe, take care of her.

JOE. She'll be all right. Stop worrying about her. She's
at the St. Francis Hotel. Now, look. Take a cab to Town-
send and Fourth. You'll see the big sign. Keith Motor
Transport Company. He'll be waiting for you.

TOM. O.K., Joe. (*trying hard*) Thanks, Joe.

JOE. Don't be silly. Get going. (*TOM goes out* R.
LADY starts puffing on cigar. As TOM goes, WESLEY

and HARRY come in together, R., and cross to piano on stage.)

NICK. (*enters from rear C. and goes behind bar*) Where the hell have you been? We've got to have some entertainment around here. Can't you see them fine people from uptown? (*He points at the LADY and MAN.*)

WESLEY. You said to come back at ten for the second show.

NICK. Did I say that?

WESLEY. Yes, sir, Mr. Nick, that's exactly what you said.

HARRY. Was the first show all right?

NICK. That wasn't a show. There was no one here to see it. How can it be a show when no one sees it? People are afraid to come down to the waterfront.

HARRY. Yeah. We were just down to Pier 27. One of the longshoremen and a cop had a fight and the cop hit him over the head with a blackjack. We saw it happen, didn't we?

WESLEY. Yes, sir, we was standing there looking when it happened.

NICK. (*crossing from behind bar to C.*) Anything else happen?

WESLEY. They was all talking.

HARRY. A man in a big car came up and said there was going to be a meeting right away and they hoped to satisfy everybody and stop the strike.

WESLEY. Right away. *Tonight.*

NICK. Well, it's about time. Them poor cops are liable to get nervous and—shoot somebody. (*to HARRY*) Come back here. I want you to tend bar for a while. I'm going to take a walk over to the pier.

HARRY. Yes, sir. (*crossing above to back of bar*)

NICK. (*to the LADY and MAN*) You society people made up your minds yet?

LADY. Have you champagne?

NICK. (*indicating JOE*) What do you think he's pouring out of that bottle, water or something?

LADY. Have you a chill bottle?

NICK. I've got a dozen of them chilled. He's been drinking champagne here all day and all night for a month now.

LADY. May we have a bottle?

NICK. It's six dollars.

LADY. I think we can manage.

MAN. I don't know. I *know* I don't know. (*NICK takes off his coat and helps HARRY into it. HARRY takes a bottle of champagne and two glasses to the LADY and the MAN, collects six dollars, and goes back behind the bar. NICK gets his coat and hat.*)

NICK. (*to WESLEY*) Rattle the keys a little, son. Rattle the keys.

WESLEY. Yes, sir, Mr. Nick. (*Starts piano*)

(*NICK is on his way out* R. *The ARAB enters and goes up to his chair.*)

NICK. Hi-ya, *Mahmed.*

ARAB. No foundation.

NICK. All the way down the line. (*He goes out. WESLEY is at the piano, playing quietly. The ARAB swallows a glass of beer, takes out his harmonica, and begins to play. WESLEY fits his playing to the ARAB's.*)

(*KITTY DUVAL, strangely beautiful, in new clothes, comes in* R. *She walks shyly, as if she were embarrassed by the fine clothes, as if she had no right to wear them. The LADY and MAN are very impressed. HARRY looks at her with amazement. JOE is reading* Time *magazine. KITTY goes to his table.*

*JOE looks up from the magazine, without the least
amazement.*)

JOE. Hello, Kitty.

KITTY. Hello, Joe.

JOE. It's nice seeing you.

KITTY. I came in a cab.

JOE. You been crying again? (*KITTY can't answer. To
HARRY:*) Bring a glass. (*HARRY comes over with a glass
and returns to bar. JOE pours KITTY a drink.*)

KITTY. I've got to talk to you.

JOE. Have a drink.

KITTY. I've never been in burlesque. We were just
poor.

JOE. Sit down, Kitty.

KITTY. (*sits down* L. *of* C. *table*) I tried other things.

JOE. Here's to you, Katerina Koranovsky. Here's to
you. And Tom.

KITTY. (*sorrowfully*) Where *is* Tom?

JOE. He's getting a job tonight driving a truck. He'll be
back in a couple of days.

KITTY. (*sadly*) I told him I'd marry him.

JOE. He wanted to see you and say good-by.

KITTY. He's too good for me. He's like a little boy.
(*wearily*) I'm — Too many things have happened to me.

JOE. Kitty Duval, you're one of the few truly innocent
people I have ever known. He'll be back in a couple of
days. Go back to the hotel and wait for him.

KITTY. That's what I mean. I can't stand being alone.
I'm no good. I tried very hard. I don't know what it is. I
miss — (*She gestures.*)

JOE. (*gently*) Do you really want to come back here,
Kitty?

KITTY. I don't know. I'm not sure. Everything *smells*
different. I don't know how I feel, or what to think.

(*gesturing pathetically*) I know I don't belong there. It's what I've wanted all my life, but it's too *late*. I try to be happy about it, but all I can do is remember everything and cry.

JOE. I don't know what to tell you, Kitty. I didn't mean to hurt you.

KITTY. You haven't hurt me. You're the only person who's ever been good to me. I've never known anybody like you. I'm not sure about love any more, but I know I love you, and I know I love Tom.

JOE. I love you, Kitty Duval.

KITTY. He'll want babies. I know he will. I know *I* will, too. Of course I will. I can't — (*She shakes her head.*)

JOE. Tom's a baby himself. You'll be happy together. He wants you to ride with him in the truck. Tom's good for you. You're good for Tom.

KITTY. Do you want me to go back and wait for him?

JOE. I can't *tell* you what to do. I think it would be a good idea, though.

KITTY. I wish I could tell you how it makes me feel to be alone. It's almost worse.

JOE. It might take a whole week, Kitty. (*He looks at her sharply, at the arrival of an idea.*) Didn't you speak of reading a book? A book of poems?

KITTY. I didn't know what I was saying.

JOE. (*trying to get up*) Of course you knew. I think you'll like poetry. Wait here a minute, Kitty. I'll go see if I can find some books.

KITTY. All right, Joe. (*He walks out of the place* R., *trying very hard not to wobble. KITTY looks at LADY and they exchange smiles.*)

(*Fog-horn. Music. The NEWSBOY comes in* R., *looks for JOE.*)

NEWSBOY. Paper?

MAN. No.

NEWSBOY. (*goes to the ARAB*) Paper, Mister?

ARAB. No foundation.

NEWSBOY. What?

ARAB. (*very angry*) No foundation.

NEWSBOY. (*starts out, turns, looks at the ARAB, shakes head*) No foundation? How do you figure? (*He goes out* R. *as BLICK and TWO COPS enter. The COPS go to bar. To BLICK:*) Paper, Mister? (*BLICK pushes him aside. The NEWSBOY goes out* R.)

BLICK. Where's Nick?

HARRY. He went for a walk.

BLICK. Who are you?

HARRY. Harry.

BLICK. (*to the ARAB who is playing harmonica*) Hey, you. Shut up. (*The ARAB stops playing and exits* R. *WESLEY looks around, stops playing.*)

BLICK. (*studies KITTY, crosses to* R. *of her*) What's your name, sister?

KITTY. (*looking at him*) Kitty Duval. What's it to you? (*KITTY's voice is now like it was at the beginning of the play: tough, independent, bitter and hard.*)

BLICK. (*angry*) Don't give me any of your gutter lip. Just answer my questions.

KITTY. You go to hell, you.

BLICK. (*coming over, enraged*) Where do you live?

KITTY. The New York Hotel. Room 21.

BLICK. Where do you work?

KITTY. I'm not working just now. I'm looking for work. (*lights cigarette*)

BLICK. What kind of work? (*KITTY can't answer.*) What kind of work? (*KITTY can't answer.*) (*furiously*) What kind of work?

KIT CARSON. (*comes over to* R. *of* C. *table*) You can't talk to a lady that way in *my* presence. (*BLICK turns and stares at KIT. The COPS begin to move from the bar to back of KIT CARSON.*)

BLICK. (*to the COPS*) It's all right, boys. I'll take care of this. (*to KIT*) What'd you say?

KIT CARSON. You got no right to hurt people. Who are *you*? (*BLICK, without a word, takes KIT out* R. *to the street. Sounds of a blow and a groan. BLICK returns with his face flushed.*)

BLICK. (*to the COPS*) O.K., boys. You can go now. Take care of him. Put him on his feet and tell him to behave himself from now on. (*to KITTY again*) Now answer my question. What kind of work?

KITTY. (*quietly*) I'm a whore, you son of a bitch. You know what kind of work I do. And I know what kind you do.

MAN. (*rises, shocked and really hurt*) Excuse me, officer, but it seems to me that your attitude —

BLICK. Shut up.

MAN. (*quietly*) — is making the poor child say things that are not true.

BLICK. Shut up, I said.

LADY. Well. (*to the MAN*) Are you going to stand for such insolence?

BLICK. (*He crosses below to* R. *of LADY. To MAN, who is standing:*) Are you?

MAN. I'll get a divorce. I'll start life all over again. Come on. Get the hell out of here! (*The MAN hurries his LADY out of the place, BLICK watching them go. To* L. *of KITTY.*)

BLICK. (*to KITTY*) Now. Let's begin again, and see that you tell the truth. What's your name?

KITTY. Kitty Duval.

BLICK. Where do you live?

KITTY. Until this evening I lived at the New York Hotel. Room 21. This evening I moved to the St. Francis Hotel.

BLICK. Oh. To the St. Francis Hotel. Nice place. Where do you work?

KITTY. I'm looking for work.

BLICK. What kind of work do you do?

KITTY. I'm an actress.

BLICK. I see. What movies have I seen you in?

KITTY. I've worked in burlesque.

BLICK. You're a liar.

KITTY. (*pathetically, as at the beginning of the play*) It's the truth.

BLICK. What are you doing here?

KITTY. I came to see if I could get a job here.

BLICK. Doing what?

KITTY. Singing—and—dancing.

BLICK. You can't sing or dance. What are you lying for?

KITTY. I can. I sang and danced in burlesque all over the country.

BLICK. You're a liar.

KITTY. I said lines, too.

BLICK. So you danced in burlesque?

KITTY. Yes.

BLICK. All right. Let's see what you did.

KITTY. I can't. There's no music, and I haven't got the right clothes.

BLICK. There's music. (*To WESLEY*) Put a nickel in that phonograph. Come on. Put a nickel in that phonograph. (*WESLEY does so. #7. To KITTY:*) All right. Get up on that stage and do a hot little burlesque number. Get going, now. Let's see you dance the way you did in burlesque, all over the country. (*KITTY goes up on stage sings a few lines and then tries to do a burlesque dance. It is beautiful in a tragic way, tragic and incredible.*) All right, start taking them off! (*KITTY removes her hat and starts to remove her jacket. JOE enters R., crosses to C.*)

JOE. (*hurrying to KITTY*) Get down from there. (*He takes KITTY into his arms. She is crying. To BLICK:*) What the hell do you think you're doing!

WESLEY. It's that man, Blick. *He* made her take off her clothes. He beat up the old man, too. (*BLICK pushes WESLEY off up C. and begins beating him.*)

TOM. (*enters R.*) What's the matter, Joe? What happened?

JOE. Is the truck out there?

TOM. Yeah, but what's happened? Kitty's crying again!

JOE. You driving to San Diego?

TOM. Yeah, Joe. But what's he doing to that poor colored boy?

JOE. Get going. Here's some money. Everything's O.K. (*to KITTY*) Dress in the truck. Take these books.

WESLEY'S VOICE. You can't hurt me. You'll get yours. You wait and see.

TOM. Joe, he's hurting that boy. I'll kill him!

JOE. Get out of here! Get married in San Diego. I'll see you when you get back. (*TOM and KITTY exit R. NICK enters and stands at the lower end of bar. JOE takes the revolver out of his pocket, looks at it.*) I've always wanted to kill somebody, but I never knew who it should be. (*He cocks the revolver, stands real straight, holds it in front of him firmly and walks to the C. door. NICK exits R. He stands a moment watching BLICK, aims very carefully, and pulls trigger. There is no shot. He cocks the pistol again and again presses the trigger. Again there is no*

shot. NICK and MCCARTHY come in R. *JOE is cocking
the pistol again. NICK runs over and grabs the gun, and
takes JOE aside.*)

NICK. What the hell do you think you're doing?

JOE. (*casually, as if it were nothing*) That dumb Tom.
Buys a six-shooter that won't even shoot once. (*NICK
hides the gun in a hurry. BLICK comes out up* C., *panting
for breath.*)

NICK. (*looks at BLICK, infuriated*) Blick! I told you to
stay out of here! Now get out of here. (*starts to push
BLICK off* R.) If you come back again, I'm going to take
you in that room where you've been beating up that
colored boy, and I'm going to murder you — slowly —
with my hands. Beat it! (*He pushes BLICK out* R. *to
HARRY:*) Go take care of the colored boy. (*HARRY
runs out* C. *WILLIE returns and doesn't sense that anything is changed. WILLIE puts another nickel into the
machine, but he does so very violently. The consequence
of this violence is that the flag comes up again. WILLIE,
amazed, stands at attention and salutes. The flag goes
down. He shakes his head.*)

WILLIE. (*thoughtfully*) As far as I'm concerned, this is
the *only* country in the world. If you ask me, *nuts* to
Europe! (*He is about to push the slide in again when the
flag comes up again. Furiously, to NICK, while he salutes
and stands at attention, pleadingly:*) Hey, Nick. This
machine is out of order.

NICK. (*somberly*) Give it a whack on the side. (*WIL-
LIE does so. A hell of a whack. The result is the flag
comes up and down, and WILLIE keeps saluting.*)

WILLIE. (*saluting*) Hey, Nick. Something's wrong.
(*The machine quiets down abruptly. WILLIE very
stealthily slides a new nickel in, and starts a new game.*)

(*From a distance THREE SHOTS are heard, each carefully timed, NICK runs out* R. *followed by MCCARTHY. The NEWSBOY enters* R., *crosses to JOE's table, senses something is wrong.*)

NEWSBOY. (*softly*) Paper, Mister? (*JOE takes them all, hands him money, shoves them off the table to floor without glancing at them.*)

(*ARAB enters* R., *picks up paper, throws it down, crosses up* R., *sits down. DRUNK enters* R.; *goes to bar. NEWSBOY backs to* C., *wishes he could cheer JOE up, notices phonograph, goes to it and puts coin in it hoping it will make JOE happier. NEWSBOY sits down,* L., *he watches JOE.*
Music begins "Missouri Waltz," Version # 4.)

NICK. (*enters, crosses to JOE*) Joe, Blick's dead! Somebody just shot him, and none of the cops are trying to find out who. (*JOE looks up slowly. Shouting:*)

JOE. (*looking up*) What?

NICK. Blick's dead.

JOE. Blick? Dead? Good! That God damn gun wouldn't go off. I *told* Tom to get a good one.

NICK. (*picking up gun and looking at it*) Joe, you wanted to kill that guy! (*HARRY returns up* C.) I'm going to buy you a bottle of champagne. (*NICK goes to bar. JOE rises, takes hat from rack, puts coat on. The NEWSBOY jumps up, helps JOE with coat.*)

NICK. What's the matter, Joe?

(*WARN curtain*)

JOE. Nothing. Nothing.

NICK. How about the champagne?

JOE. Thanks. (*crosses to* C.)

NICK. It's not eleven yet. Where are you going, Joe?

JOE. I don't know. Nowhere.

NICK. Will I see you tomorrow?

JOE. I don't know. I don't think so. (*KIT CARSON enters* R., *walks to JOE.*) Somebody just shot a man. How are you feeling?

KIT. Never felt better in my life. (*quietly*) I shot a man once. In San Francisco. Shot him two times. In 1939, I think it was. In October. Fellow named Blick or Glick or something like that. Couldn't stand the way he talked to ladies. Went up to my room and got my old pearl-handled revolver and waited for him on Pacific Street. Saw him walking, and let him have it, two times. Had to throw the beautiful revolver into the Bay. (*HARRY, NICK, the ARAB and the DRUNK close in around him. JOE walks slowly to the stairs leading to the street, turns and waves. Exits.*)

CURTAIN

PROPERTY PLOT

ACT ONE

Bar, with iced ¼ keg of beer and tap:

Glass and beer scraper
Quart bottle of rye and shot glass
2 dish towels
1 dish rag
1 apron
1 ash tray with matches
1 basket of pretzels
1 copy of "Daily Racing Form"
1 glass of beer (up end)
4 false beer glasses
2 false beer steins
Small tray
1 Bottle of champagne (hot tea)
2 Bottles of champagne (cold tea)

Back Bar:

8 champagne glasses
3 shot glasses
2 menus
30 nickels
2 practical rye bottles
Nick's hat and coat
Dress glasses and bottles ad lib.

ACT TWO

Strike:

Deck of cards

Coat from piano
Newspapers
Bottle of champagne and 2 glasses from table L.C.

Set:

Rye bottle ⎫
Highball glass ⎬   table C.
Shot glass ⎭
Bottle of champagne (hot) ⎫
Champagne glass ⎬   table L.C.
L.C. table to new marks.

OFF RIGHT:

Atlas (TOM)
.38 Cal. Revolver, boxed (TOM)
7   .38 cartridges boxed (TOM)
Cigar stub (KIT)
Harmonica (ARAB)

ACT THREE

Bed:

Covers
Pillow
Small Book
Picture
High Stool
Coin telephone
Telephone Book
Coat hook — L. of telephone with Joe's coat
Marble game (electric)
Phonograph

3 24″ square tables
6 bentwood chairs
1 bentwood chair on 2″ platform (up of bar)
3 ashtrays with matches (on each table)
1 basket of pretzels (L. table)
Deck of cards (L.C. table)
Upright piano (cover off and in tune to 440 "A")
1 bentwood chair (piano platform)
1 copy of "Readers Digest" (piano)
2 sheets manuscript music paper (piano)
2 dance mats (small stage)

OFF RIGHT:

Address Book (DUDLEY)
Cigarette Case (KITTY)
Package with 2 dolls, 3 whistles, 1 music box (TOM)
Rubber black-jack (BLICK)
4 slug nickels (DUDLEY)
4 slug nickels (JOE)
25 paper bills (JOE)
5 paper bills (NICK)
5 papers (NEWSBOY)
1 slug nickel (SAILOR)

Table:

Mirror (hand)
Glass
Dress ad lib

Trench coat on nail L. of door
2 rag rugs
Practical door slam (off L.)

ACT FOUR

Strike:

Atlas
Cartridges
Champagne bottle } table L.C.
Champagne glass
Beer stein

Set:

Preset three glasses of beer (bar)

ACT FIVE

Strike:

Beer glass table L.

Set:

Atlas (open)
.38 Revolver
Cartridges
3 cigarettes } table C.
Bottle of champagne (hot)
Champagne glass

Bar:

2 practical bottles of champagne (cold)
6 Champagne glasses

Off right

25 newspapers (NEWSBOY)
1 slug nickel (NEWSBOY)
Copy of "Life"
Copy of "Liberty"   TOM
Copy of "Time"
Cellophane bag of jelly-beans
7 packages of Gum
6 Wheeling stogies   JOE
3 books
Bills (GENTLEMAN)

Sound

.22 blank revolver and cover gun
Ratchet
Gong   } Pin-Ball Effect

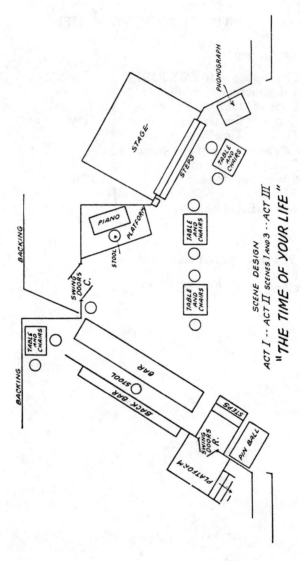

SCENE DESIGN
ACT I -- ACT II SCENES 1 AND 3 -- ACT III
"THE TIME OF YOUR LIFE"